# Matter & Materials

## Grades 1-3

Written by Miranda Palmer
Illustrated by Ric Ward

ISBN 1-55035-673-9
Copyright 2001
Revised December 2005
All Rights Reserved • Printed in Canada

Published in the United States by:
On the Mark Press
3909 Witmer Road PMB 175
Niagara Falls, New York
14305
www.onthemarkpress.com

Published in Canada by:
S&S Learning Materials
15 Dairy Avenue
Napanee, Ontario
K7R 1M4
www.sslearning.com

# Look For OTHER SCIENCE UNITS

# Matter and Materials

## Table of Contents

# Matter and Materials

## Overall Expectations

Students will:

- distinguish between objects and materials.
- identify and describe the properties of some materials.
- investigate the properties of materials.
- make appropriate use of materials when designing and making objects.
- describe the function of specific materials in manufactured objects that they use in daily life.
- demonstrate an understanding of the properties of familiar liquids and solids, and of interactions between them.
- identify ways in which we use our knowledge of liquids and solids to make useful objects.
- demonstrate an understanding of the properties of materials that can be magnetized or charged.
- identify and describe, through observation, ways in which static electric charges are made in common materials.
- identify different types of interactions that take place between both charged and magnetized materials.
- identify familiar uses of magnets and give examples of commonly created static electric charges.

## Specific Expectations

### Grade One:

By the end of grade one, students will:

- identify each of the senses and demonstrate an understanding of how the senses help us to recognize and use a variety of materials.
- describe various materials, using information gathered by their senses.
- identify properties of materials that are important to the function of objects.
- describe, using their observations, ways in which materials can be changed to alter their appearance, smell and texture.

# Matter and Materials

## Grade Two:

By the end of grade two, students will:

- describe, through observation, the properties of liquids and solids.
- distinguish between solids that dissolve in water and solids that do not.
- describe, through observation, the characteristics of the three states of water, and identify the conditions that cause changes from one state to another.
- recognize that liquid and solid states remain constant in some circumstances.
- identify reversible changes in materials.
- identify, through observation, various substances that are buoyant, absorbent, or soluble.
- evaluate the appropriateness of the materials chosen in the design and construction of a structure that is intended to float.

## Grade Three:

By the end of grade three, students will:

- classify, through observation, materials that are magnetic and non-magnetic, and identify materials that can be magnetized.
- identify, through observation, the effect of various conditions on the strength of magnets and on static electric charges in materials.
- compare different materials by measuring their magnetic strength or the strength of their electric charge.
- identify, through observation, pairs of materials that produce a charge when rubbed together.
- describe and demonstrate how some magnetized or electrically charged materials may either push or pull similar materials.
- determine, through observation, how to test a magnet's polarity.
- identify materials that can be placed between a magnet and an attracted object without diminishing the strength of the attraction.
- predict, verify, and describe the interaction of two objects that are similarly charged.
- describe, through observation, changes in the force of attraction at different distances, for both magnetic and static electric forces.

# Matter and Materials

## Teacher Information

### What is matter?

Matter is the substance from which all things are made. All objects are made of matter and may differ widely from one another. All objects have one thing in common – they all occupy space. Matter is defined by scientists as anything that occupies space. All matter has *inertia* – an ability to resist any change in its condition of rest or of motion. The amount of matter in an object is called its *mass*. Scientists define *mass* as *a measure of inertia*. The earth's gravitational attraction for a given mass gives matter its *weight*.

Matter can be changed into energy; energy can be changed into matter. Matter changes into energy when radium or other radioactive elements disintegrate (e.g. an atomic bomb explosion). Energy changes into matter when subatomic particles collide at high speeds and create new, heavier particles.

### The Properties of Matter

There are many varieties of matter, each variety possessing certain common characteristics. Each variety is described by its special characteristics or *properties*. These properties make one type of matter different from others. Matter has two main properties -- *physical* and *chemical*.

### Physical Properties:

Certain types of matter are recognized by our *sight, smell, touch, taste* or *hearing*. Silver is recognized by its color; salt by its taste; gasoline by its odor. These are examples of physical properties of matter. Another property is *density*, the amount of mass per volume. For example, a block of cork weighs less than a comparably sized block of wood. Another property is *solubility* – the ability to dissolve. *Conductivity* is a property that describes matter's ability to conduct heat or electricity.

### Chemical Properties:

Chemical properties of matter reveal how a substance acts when it undergoes chemical change. For example, one chemical property of iron is its ability to combine with oxygen in moist air to form *iron oxide* or rust. Scientists call changes in the composition of matter *chemical changes*. Changes that alter the value of physical properties, such as weight or density, but cause no change in the composition of matter are called *physical changes*. For example, when water changes to steam it undergoes a physical not chemical change.

# Matter and Materials

## Compounds and Elements:

Scientists are able to separate a substance into two or more simpler kinds of matter with new properties, by using chemical processes. This substance is called a *compound substance* or a *chemical compound*. Substances that cannot be broken down into simpler varieties of matter by chemical means are called *elementary substances*.

## Structure of Matter

Most matter is made up of *atoms*. An *atom* is the smallest amount of an element that can enter into a chemical reaction to form a compound. Atoms are made up of particles called *protons, neutrons* and *electrons*. Protons and neutrons are made up of particles called *quarks*. Quarks are held together by particles called *gluons*.

All the atoms contained in an elementary substance have identical chemical properties. A *compound substance* is formed when two or more elements are combined and the atoms of one substance combine with the atoms of another. These atoms form larger particles called *molecules*. For example, two atoms of hydrogen and one atom of oxygen form one molecule of water. Atoms and molecules are extremely small and are impossible to count.

Compound substances may be *organic* or *inorganic*. Organic compounds contain the element carbon. They are found in all living organisms. Organic molecules are among the largest molecules and may contain thousands of atoms. All other compounds are called *inorganic*.

Molecules are bound together by electrical force. This force is produced by the electrons in the atoms.

## States of Matter

Matter is usually found in three physical forms – *solid, liquid* and *gas*. For example, ice is a solid state but when heated it melts at a definite temperature to form a liquid called water. Heat may also raise the temperature of the water to a boiling point, producing steam, a gas. When the heat is removed the process is reversed. The chemical composition of water remains the same regardless of its changes of state. *Plasma* is a fourth state of matter, existing only under special conditions.

## Solids:

All solids have *form, hardness* and *rigidity* (the ability to oppose a change of shape). For example, a stone does not easily change shape. Some solids are brittle and will shatter when struck. Others have great *tensile* strength and resist being pulled apart. Solid metals have *malleability* (the ability to be beaten thin) and *ductility* (the ability to be drawn into wires). The atoms in almost all solids are arranged in regular patterns called *crystals*.

# Matter and Materials

## Liquids:

Liquids have no shape of their own. They take on the shape of the container into which they are placed. They fill the container when their volume is the same as the volume of the container.

## Gases:

All gases have almost identical behavior. They exert pressure in all directions. All gases are compressible. Gases expand and exert pressure when they are confined.

## Plasmas:

Plasmas are found in such places as the interior of stars, outer space, neon lamps and some laboratory experiments. Plasmas result when the atoms in a gas become ionized or electrically charged. Electrical forces between its atoms give the gas new physical properties.

## Materials

Many manufactured products are made from solid substances called materials. There are two groups of materials: *natural* and *extracted*. Natural materials include *stone*, *wood*, and *wool*. Extracted materials include *plastics*, *alloys* (metal mixtures) and *ceramics*.

Manufacturers evaluate materials by their *properties* (qualities). Most properties of materials fall into six groups: *mechanical, chemical, electrical, magnetic, thermal* and *optical*.

## Mechanical Properties:

Some of the most important mechanical properties are: *stiffness, yield stress, toughness, strength, creep and fatigue resistance*. *Stiffness* measures how much a material bends when subjected to a mechanical force; for example, the degree to which a shelf first bends when a heavy object is placed on it. *Yield stress* measures how much force per unit area must be exerted on a material for that material to permanently deform (change its shape). Materials that deform easily are usually undesirable. *Toughness* measures a material's resistance to cracking. *Strength* measures the greatest force a material can withstand without breaking. *Creep* is a measure of a material's resistance to gradual deformation under a constant force. *Fatigue resistance* measures the resistance of a material to repeated applications and withdrawals of force.

## Chemical Properties:

*Catalytic* properties measure the ability of a material to function as a *catalyst* (its ability to provide a favorable site for a certain chemical reaction to occur). *Resistance to corrosion* measures how well a material holds up to chemical attack by the environment.

# Matter and Materials

## Electrical Properties:

Certain electrical properties are necessary in order to produce products designed either to *conduct* (carry) or *block* the flow of electrical current.

## Magnetic Properties:

Magnetic properties describe a material's response to a *magnetic field*. (e.g. the region around a magnet or a conductor where the *force of magnetism* can be felt.)

## Thermal Properties:

Thermal properties reflect a material's response to heat. *Thermal conductivity* measures how well a material conducts heat. For example, pots and pans must be made of materials that have a high *thermal conductivity* so they may transfer heat to food. *Heat capacity* measures a material's ability to contain heat. This property is important in the production of insulation materials.

## Optical Properties:

Optical properties describe how a material responds to light. The degree to which a material changes the direction of a beam of light passing through it is important in the manufacture of glass lenses . The less light a material absorbs, the more transparent the material.

## Natural Materials

Natural materials are usually used as they are found. They may be cleaned, cut or processed in a manner that does not require much energy. Stone and biological materials are natural materials.

## Stone:

Strong, hard types of rock are used as *building stone*. There are two types of stone: *crushed* and *dimensional*. Crushed stone is mixed with tar-like substances to make *asphalt*, a paving material. It is also mixed with cement and sand to make *concrete*. Limestone and granite are found in crushed stone. *Dimensional stone* is used in finishing and decorating buildings. Granite, limestone, marble, sandstone and slate are used as building stone.

## Biological Materials:

*Biological materials* are substances that are parts of a plant or animal. *Wood* is an important biological material because of its strength, toughness and low density. Thousands of products are made from wood, such as houses, boats, furniture, and railroad ties. It is also used as a raw material for a wide variety of products such as paper, rayon and charcoal.

# Matter and Materials

*Plant fibers* from cotton, flax and jute are often used in their natural state. Most plant fibers are flexible and may be spun into yarn.

*Leather* is a tough, flexible material made from the skins of animals. Shoes, belts, baseball gloves, baseballs, basketballs and footballs are made from leather. *Suede*, a soft leather, is used in making clothing.

*Animal fibers* include fur, wool and silk. These materials are excellent insulators and are used in making clothing. Silk is the strongest natural fiber and is made from silkworm cocoons. Clothing and decorative fabrics are often made from silk.

## Extracted Materials

*Extracted materials* are created through energy intensive processes that may alter the microstructures of the substances. Extracted materials include ceramics, metals and their alloys, plastics, rubber, composite materials and semiconductors.

*Ceramic materials* include brick, cement, glass and porcelain. They are made from clay, feldspar, silica and talc. Ceramic products include dinnerware, bathroom fixtures, building materials, insulators for electric power lines, windows, and lenses for microscopes.

For thousands of years, people have used such *metals* as copper, gold, iron and silver. Today, metals are important in all aspects of construction and manufacturing. They are strong, and good conductors of heat and electric current. Pure copper is used in electrical wiring.

When metals are too soft in their pure form, they are used as ingredients in *alloys*. Stainless steel, cast iron and wrought iron are all alloys of iron. Certain elements mixed with steel give it such properties as resisting corrosion, increasing its hardness or making it more resistant to heat.

*Plastics* are synthetic materials made up of molecular chains called *polymers*. There are two types of plastics: *thermosets* and *thermoplastics*. Thermosets can be heated and set only once. They are highly resistant to heat and are used for electrical parts, insulation foam, oven gaskets and appliance handles. Thermosets are also used in luggage and automobile parts. Thermoplastics can be melted and reshaped. Their use is more wide-spread than thermosets. Common thermoplastic products are telephone bodies, packaging and bottles.

*Natural rubber* comes from the sap of rubber trees. *Synthetic rubber* is made from petroleum. Rubber is made of *polymers* that stretch easily and then return to their original shape. This property is called *elasticity*. Rubber's elasticity is able to make it tough, hold air, and keep out water. Tires, tubes and waterproof clothing are made from rubber.

# Matter and Materials

*Composite materials* are made by artificially combining a large amount of one substance with fibers, flakes or layers of another substance. *Fiberglass* consists of glass fibers and a *polymer* such as *epoxy*. Fiberglass composites are used to produce products such as automobile bodies, fishing rods, aircraft parts, tennis rackets, and golf clubs.

Semiconductors are materials that conduct electricity more freely than insulators, but not as well as conductors. Pure cells of semiconductor material, combined with small, and controlled amounts of other substances, may perform many electronic functions. Silicon crystals are the building blocks of computer chips.

## Bonding

*Bonding* is a force that attracts atoms to one another and holds them together. Such forces depend upon the electron structure of the atoms. *Chemical bonds* are either *ionic, covalent* or *metallic*. *Ionic* bonds are created by the transfer of electrons from one atom to one or more atoms. The atom that loses electrons becomes a positive ion. The atoms that gain electrons become negative ions. In *covalent bonding*, two or more atoms share pairs of electrons. A shared pair consists of one electron from each of the two atoms. During *metallic bonding*, all the atoms in a metal crystal share electrons. The shared electrons are able to move freely throughout the crystal. The metal nuclei are surrounded and held together by the movement of negative electrons. *Physical bonds* known as *van der Waals forces* hold molecules together in a group. *Van der Waals* forces are electrical forces carried by an interaction between charges of neighboring molecules. They are much weaker than chemical bonds because no transfer or sharing of electrons occurs.

## List of Vocabulary

The following words may be recorded in alphabetical order on a chart. Check off or star each of the following words as it is introduced or used throughout the theme:

atom, bumpy, change, cotton, electricity, flexible, fur, gas, hard, hearing, heavy,

liquid, materials, matter, mass, metals, molecules, object, plastic, properties,

rough, rubber, shiny, sight, smell, smooth, soft, solid, spongy, static, taste. tough,

weight, wood, wool

# Matter and Materials
## Teaching Suggestions

This comprehensive primary unit covers many topics in matter and materials that are taught from grades one to three. Methods of assessment may include formal testing, evaluation of charts and graphs, ability to follow instructions and recording anecdotal observations.

This unit strives to give students a basic understanding of matter, materials and reversible changes of state. Lessons are designed to reach all types of learners, showing them how to apply the information to the primary world. In the process, investigative methods of discovery and experimentation are introduced. Consequently, students must use their skills of observation and draw conclusions while experimenting with different materials.

Although materials needed for this unit may be readily available in school, a few items must be prepared ahead of time in order to be ready for student use. For many of these activities, the teacher needs to set up the lesson before the class begins.

You may wish to do only three or four experiments per day. It is suggested that you divide the experiments into groups of solids with solids, liquids with liquids, and liquids with solids so students make the connection that liquids will always mix well, some solids will mix with liquids, and solids will not usually mix with other solids.

Teachers may wish to have each student create a vocabulary list at the back of the notebook, in addition to a definitions page. Journaling is encouraged on a regular basis to help the students apply what they learn in the classroom to their daily lives.

Teachers will need to take the first five to ten minutes to explain the input sections of the lesson and then explain how to do the activity. Where reading skills are low or the vocabulary is beyond the range of some students, the activities may be done collectively or in small groups.

If the quiz at the end of this unit is too challenging for your students, the activities called "Colors Matter" and "Make a Magazine" may be useful evaluation tools. Early primary teachers may find these more useful because the instructions may be given verbally with no written work required from the student.

Questions at the end of the activities may be used for class discussion or assigned as homework, depending on the students' writing skills.

In all cases, the activities are designed so that students may read the instructions on their own. Instructions may also be read out by the teacher, to help the students move from step to step.

# Activity: Simon Says

## Purpose:

This activity will help introduce or refresh the ideas of solids, liquids and gases. It is recommended that you clear a large area or take your class outside for this game.

## Procedure:

This game is played like the traditional "Simon Says" game except the teacher in this activity will name something that is either a solid, a liquid or a gas. The children need to decide if the item stated is either a solid, a liquid or a gas, and become molecules in that item.

In order to play the game, teach the students that when you say, "Simon says solids" or name something that is a solid, they should all pack together tightly and stand as still as possible. Naming something that is "liquid", the children should join hands and sway or walk so that they "flow" like a liquid. Naming a "gas", the students should bounce off each other and objects in a gentle, disorganized way. You may wish to have the students practice these first.

It is suggested that you instruct the students to stop between "Simon Says" instructions. Students are "out" if they perform the incorrect action or if they move when the teacher didn't say "Simon Says" before starting the action.

## Example:

**Teacher:** "Simon says be like a desk."

**Students:** They decide that a desk is a solid and move quickly to be as close to each other, and as still as possible, to mimic molecules of a solid.

**Teacher:** "Simon says stop!"

**Students:** Students relax and separate to wait for the next item.

## Picture Perfect Solids

Decide which of the following items are solids. <u>Color</u> only the ones that are solids. Cut them out and glue them to your **'Picture Perfect Solids'** worksheet. Try to print the names of the solids too.

## Picture Perfect Solids

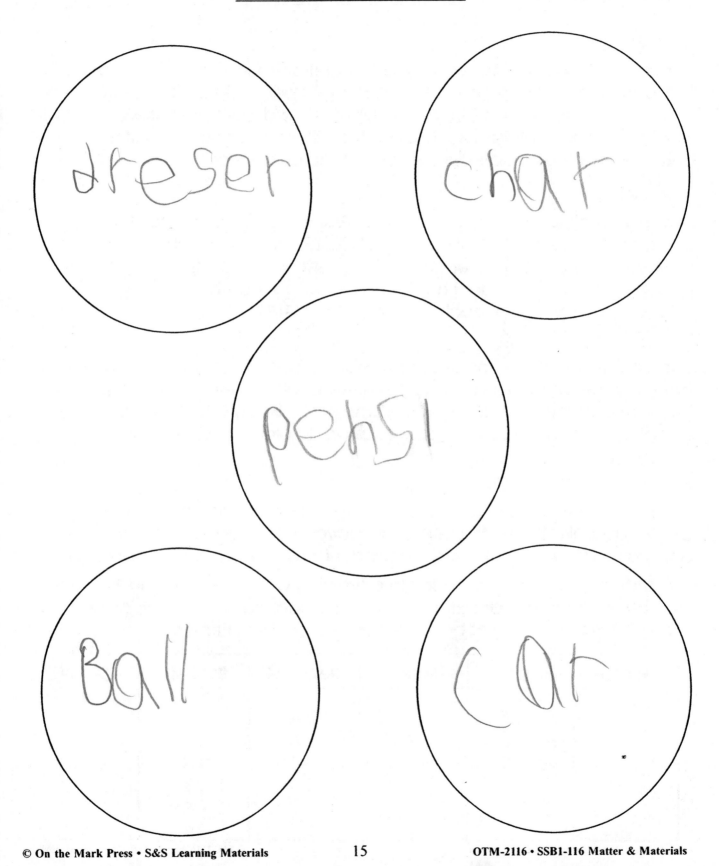

dreser

char

pehsl

Ball

car

SOFT

## Soft or Hard

HARD

## Preparation:

Before the lesson begins, you will need to set up at least six stations around the classroom. You will need one solid object per station. Choose items that have at least one of the following attributes: hard, shiny, soft, flexible, smooth or rough. Make sure that each attribute is represented at least once, even if the objects contain more than one attribute.

## Procedure:

Divide your class into six equal groups. Assign each group one of the following names: HARD, SHINY, SOFT, FLEXIBLE, SMOOTH, ROUGH. Photocopy and laminate enough of the 'attribute tags' from the following pages so that each student has at least one tag that shows the group's attribute. For example, each student in the HARD group should have a tag that says HARD.

Each group will move from object to object, deciding if the item has the particular attribute. If it does, students are to place one of their tags beside the item and then move on. For example, a mirror is hard, shiny and smooth, so each group with those tags would place one of its tags beside the mirror.

## Follow-Up:

After the classifying activity, make a large chart on the chalkboard or on chart paper like the example below. Have the students brainstorm different objects that fit into each category and record their names on the chart.

You may also use the reproducible classifying worksheet provided on page 19. The students will cut out objects from magazines and catalogs and paste them in the correct boxes under their correct attributes.

| HARD | SOFT | SHINY | SMOOTH | ROUGH | FLEXIBLE |
|------|------|-------|--------|-------|----------|
|      |      |       |        |       |          |

| HARD | SOFT |
|------|------|
| HARD | SOFT |
| HARD | SOFT |
| HARD | SOFT |
| SHINY | FLEXIBLE |
| SHINY | FLEXIBLE |

# ATTRIBUTE CARDS

| | |
|:---:|:---:|
| **SHINY** | **FLEXIBLE** |
| **SHINY** | **FLEXIBLE** |
| **SMOOTH** | **ROUGH** |
| **SMOOTH** | **ROUGH** |
| **SMOOTH** | **ROUGH** |
| **SMOOTH** | **ROUGH** |

## Classifying Solids

Look through magazines and catalogs to find pictures of things that are solids.
Classify each one under the word that describes it.

| HARD | SOFT | SMOOTH |
|------|------|--------|
|      |      |        |
| ROUGH | FLEXIBLE | SHINY |
|       |          |       |

## Hard as a...........

Draw pictures of as many hard things as you can. Print each name under its picture. Share your pictures with a partner. Draw a picture of one thing that your partner has that you don't. These hard objects are all solids

| | | |
|---|---|---|
| _____ | _____ | _____ |
| _____ | _____ | _____ |
| _____ | _____ | _____ |
| _____ | _____ | _____ |

# Solids

 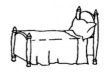

**Solids** are made up of molecules that are packed tightly together and are almost perfectly still.

Not all solids are exactly the same as other solids.

We use different solids for different things, depending on their properties.

**Cotton** is a flexible, soft solid that we use to make clothes.

**Steel** is a hard, inflexible material that we use to make cars.

Can you imagine a T-shirt made of steel or a car made of cotton?

These different types of solids are called **materials**. Solid objects are made from materials.

On the **Solids' Organizer**, we look at some of the properties of different materials.

You will need five to ten different solids,

## Examples:

| tin can, chalk, rock, paper, desk, chair leg, paper clip, ceramic bowl, clay pot, book, rope, cotton, stick of wood, etc. |
| --- |

Write the name of the item in the left column of the organizer.

Put a check mark in each column that shows a property of that item.

Note the sound it makes when tapped with a pencil.

The first one is done for you on the organizer.

## Solids Organizer

| ITEM | SHINY | DULL | HARD | SOFT | ROUGH | SMOOTH | FLEXIBLE | INFLEXIBLE | SOUND |
| --- | --- | --- | --- | --- | --- | --- | --- | --- | --- |
| Steel | ✓ | | ✓ | | | ✓ | | ✓ | ringing |
| | | | | | | | | | |
| | | | | | | | | | |
| | | | | | | | | | |
| | | | | | | | | | |

## Solids Organizer

| ITEM | SHINY | DULL | HARD | SOFT | ROUGH | SMOOTH | FLEXIBLE | INFLEXIBLE | SOUND |
|------|-------|------|------|------|-------|--------|----------|------------|-------|
| Steel | ✓ | | ✓ | | | ✓ | | ✓ | ringing |
| | | | | | | | | | |
| | | | | | | | | | |
| | | | | | | | | | |
| | | | | | | | | | |
| | | | | | | | | | |
| | | | | | | | | | |
| | | | | | | | | | |
| | | | | | | | | | |
| | | | | | | | | | |

**Matter and Materials** - Skill: The student will brainstorm and illustrate materials that are made from wood, plastic, metal and rubber.

# Materials

In the following chart, draw and name three items that are made from **wood**, three items that are made from **plastic**, three items that are made of **metal** and three items that are made of **rubber**.

| Material: Wood | | |
|---|---|---|
| **Object**<br><br>____________ | **Object**<br><br>____________ | **Object**<br><br>____________ |
| **Material: Plastic** | | |
| **Object**<br><br>____________ | **Object**<br><br>____________ | **Object**<br><br>____________ |
| | **Material: Metal** | |
| **Object**<br><br>____________ | **Object**<br><br>____________ | **Object**<br><br>____________ |
| | **Material: Rubber** | |
| **Object**<br><br>____________ | **Object**<br><br>____________ | **Object**<br><br>____________ |

**Matter and Materials** - Skill: The students will brainstorm and illustrate objects that are made from wood, plastic, metal, rubber and cotton.

## Can You Guess?

In the following chart, different materials are given. Draw and name three objects that each material is used for.

| Material | Objects |
|---|---|
| **Wood** 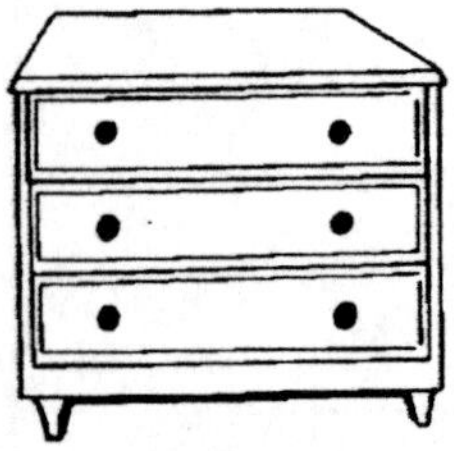 | |
| **Plastic** 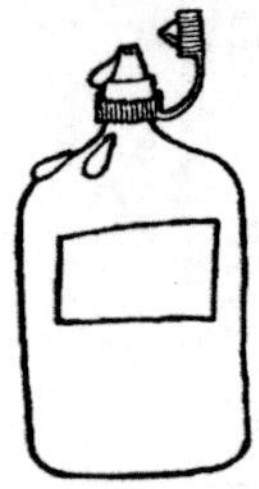 | |
| **Metal** 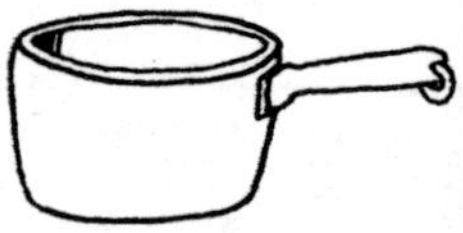 | |
| **Rubber** 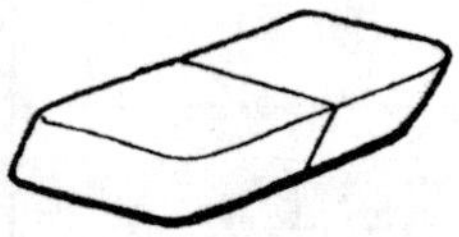 | |
| **Cotton** 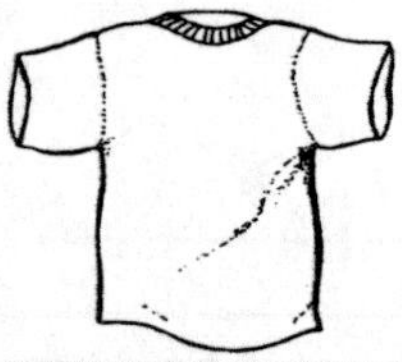 | |

# How Are Materials Used in the Classroom?

On the following chart draw five to ten objects that are found in your classroom. In the materials column, write what each one is made from. In some cases, there may be more than one material needed to make the object. List as many as you can.

| Object | Materials | Object | Materials |
|---|---|---|---|
|  |  |  |  |
|  |  |  |  |
|  |  |  |  |
|  |  |  |  |
|  |  |  |  |

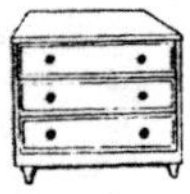

# Which Is It?

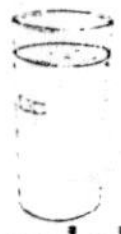

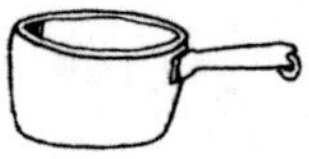

In the following chart, name the material used to make each object. Beside each material check whether it is hard like a rock or flexible like an elastic band.

| Object | Material | Hard | Flexible |
|---|---|---|---|
| Grocery Bag 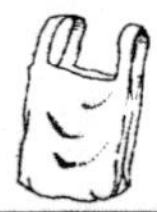 | | | |
| Plastic Wrap 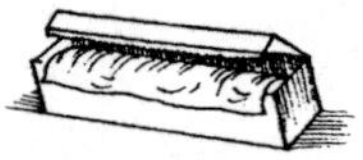 | | | |
| Tree 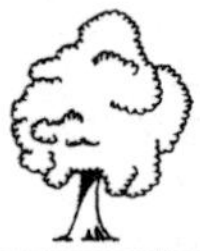 | | | |
| Pencil 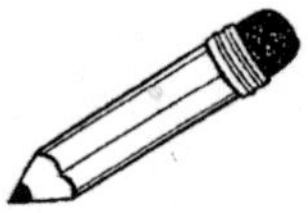 | | | |
| Eraser 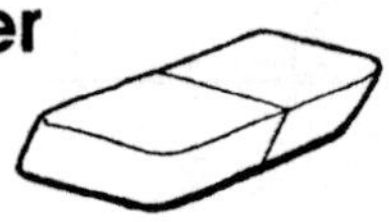 | | | |
| Tires 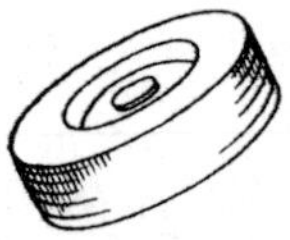 | | | |
| Car 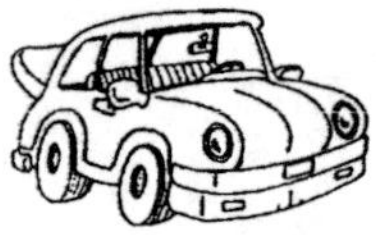 | | | |
| T-shirt 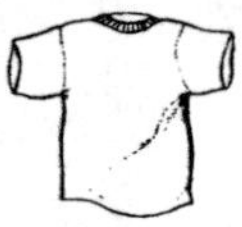 | | | |
| Pencil Box 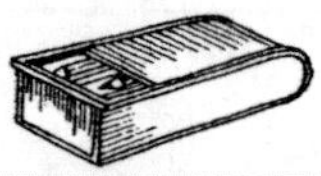 | | | |
| Window 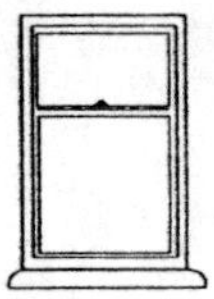 | | | |

# Which Is It?

## Questions:

Answer each question with a complete sentence.

1. Which material is both hard and flexible?

   _____

   _____

   _____

2. Why is it better to have flexible plastic for a grocery bag?

   _____

   _____

   _____

3. Why should the top of your desk be hard?

   _____

   _____

   _____

4. Why is a soft, flexible eraser better than a hard one?

   _____

   _____

   _____

5. Why is rubber, instead of wood, used to make tires?

   _____

   _____

   _____

Color the following objects. Underline the ones made from rubber.

     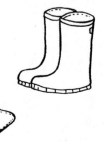

# Sink or Swim!

- For this activity, the class will need to be divided into pairs. Each pair needs a fist-sized ball of play-doh and a container of water big enough to allow the play-doh to float when it is flattened.

- First, have the students shape their play-doh into a ball and place it carefully in the water. The play-doh will sink.

- Next, have the students experiment with different shapes to see if they can get the play-doh to sink less and ultimately float. The more flat or 'boat-shaped' they can make the play-doh, the better it will float.

- This experiment can be the jumping off point for many discussions such as: Why do boats float? How does changing the shape of objects make them more or less likely to float?

- - - - - - - - - - - - - - - - ✂ cut

Circle the objects below that you know will float.

# Will It Float?

- In this experiment, you will determine if several objects will sink or float.

- Before you try the activity, make your predictions as to whether or not you think each object will float or sink.

- Do the experiment.

- Record your results on the 'Will It Float?' Chart.

- You will need the following items:

wood

flat tin foil

tin foil rolled into a ball

an eraser

bits of tissue paper

paper towels

pebbles of various sizes

toothpicks

a pencil

a plastic toy or dish

a large bucket or tub of water

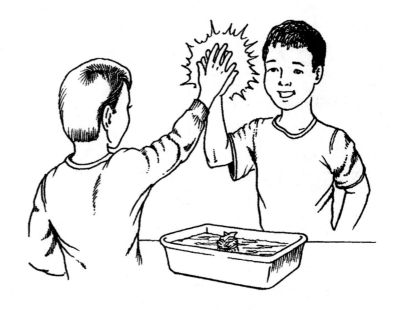

**Note:** This experiment may be completed in groups but it is best done as a whole class activity.  Have the class take a vote as to whether or not they believe the item will float.  You may want to have the students draw the results instead of recording them in charts.

## Questions for Discussion:

1. Why did the ball of tin foil float?
2. Why did the flat tin foil sink?
3. Why do you think some things float while others sink?

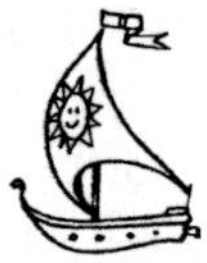

# Will It Float?

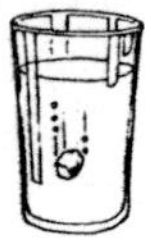

Record your predictions and results in the following chart.

| Object | Prediction (Float/Sink) | Actual Result |
|---|---|---|
| Flat Tin Foil 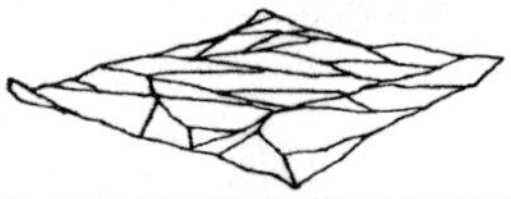 | | |
| Balled Tin Foil 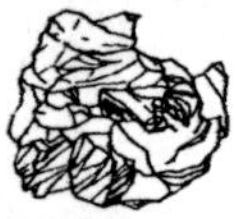 | | |
| Eraser 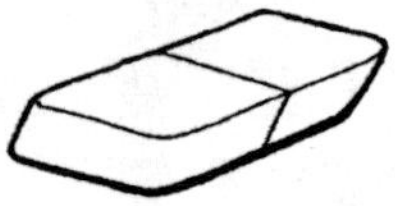 | | |
| Tissue Paper Bits 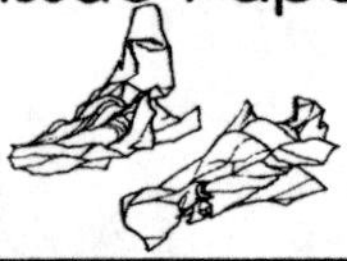 | | |
| Paper Towel 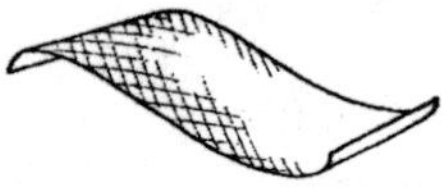 | | |
| Pebbles 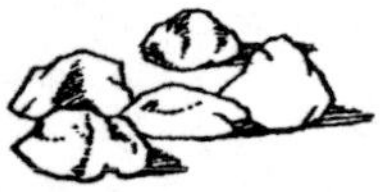 | | |
| Plastic Toy/Dish 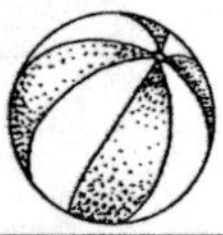 | | |
| Pencil 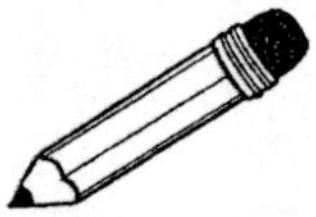 | | |
| Wood (toothpicks) 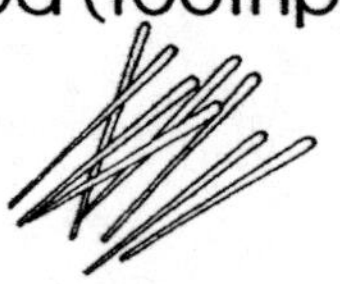 | | |

# Make It Float!

Brainstorm as many objects as you have seen floating on water.  In the box below, draw and name five objects that float.

---

### Things That Float

---

Choose one object from your list. Design a new object, using one or more materials.  Test your object by floating it for one minute in water.  In the box below, draw your design.

---

### Floating Object Design

---

1. Did your design pass the one minute test?

2. How would you change your design to make it better?  Share your ideas with a partner.

# Mixing Matters

In the following experiments, you will mix a number of solids with solids, liquids with liquids, and liquids with solids. Before you begin, make a prediction as to whether or not the two materials will mix. Then, check your predictions! Record your responses on the chart called "Mixing Matters Record Sheet" or on the picture chart called "Mixing Matters Picture Chart".

You will need:

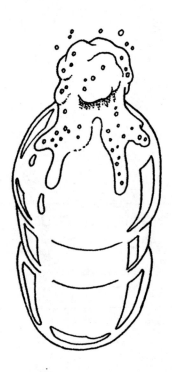

several small stones or pebbles

plastic drinking cups

sand

dirt

water

flour

cooking oil

aluminum foil

salt

sugar

warm water

stir sticks

ketchup

Mix the materials in the plastic drinking cups. Use the stir sticks to try to mix the materials together.

## Note:

This activity may either be done as a whole class activity or in groups of four to five students, where each student makes his/her own prediction and records his/her own results.

# Mixing Matters

| Materials Mixed | Will/Won't Mix | Actual Observation |
|---|---|---|
| Pebbles with Pebbles | | |
| Sand with Flour | | |
| Dirt with Water | | |
| Cooking Oil with Water | | |
| Aluminum Foil with Salt | | |
| Sugar with Water | | |
| Ketchup with Pebbles | | |
| Flour with Water | | |
| Sand with Water | | |
| Salt with Warm Water | | |
| Sugar with Warm Water | | |
| | | |
| | | |
| | | |
| | | |
| | | |

# Mixing Matters Picture Chart

Use this chart to record a picture of your observations from your mixing matters experiment.

| Materials Mixed | Will/Won't Mix | Actual Observation |
|---|---|---|
| Pebbles with Pebbles | | |
| Sand with Flour | | |
| Dirt with Water | | |
| Cooking Oil with Water | | |
| Aluminum Foil with Salt | | |
| Sugar with Water | | |

# Mixing Matters Picture Chart

Use this chart to record a picture of your observations from your mixing matters experiment.

| Materials Mixed | Will/Won't Mix | Actual Observation |
|---|---|---|
| Ketchup with Pebbles | | |
| Flour with Water | | |
| Sand with Water | | |
| Salt with Warm Water | | |
| Sugar with Warm Water | | |
| | | |

# Matter

Everything that you can touch, taste, smell and see is made up of something called "matter". Even what you can't see is still made up of matter. Scientists break the big category of matter into three smaller parts: **solids**, **liquids** and **gases**.

A **solid** is something that keeps its shape. It can be hard or soft and flexible. An example of a solid is the chair that you are sitting on.

A **liquid** is something that can be poured into another container. It takes the shape of the container. An example of a liquid is water.

A **gas** is something that is in the air. Usually you cannot see gases. An example of a gas is the air we breath. This is called oxygen.

In the following activity, decide whether the item belongs in the category of solid, liquid or gas. Put a check mark in the correct category.

| Item | Solid | Liquid | Gas | Item | Solid | Liquid | Gas |
|---|---|---|---|---|---|---|---|
| desk | | | | cup | | | |
| water | | | | steam | | | |
| air | | | | exhaust fumes | | | |
| chalkboard | | | | milk | | | |
| chair | | | | glass | | | |
| orange juice | | | | oil | | | |

# More Matter

All matter is made up of tiny particles that are too small to see without the use of a microscope. These particles are called 'molecules'.

Molecules in a solid like your desk are pressed very close together, so they don't move.

Molecules in a liquid such as water are further apart, leaving room to move and flow.

Molecules in a gas, such as the air we breathe are very far apart and bounce off each other in a disorganized or random way. When you move your hands through the air, you are making gas molecules move in a crazy way!

Finish the following sentences:

1.  Everything you can _____, _____, _____ and _____ is made up of something called _____.

2.  Scientists break the big category of matter into _____ smaller parts: _____, _____ and _____.

3.  All matter is made up of tiny particles that are _____

    _____

4.  Molecules in a solid are _____

5.  Molecules in a liquid _____

6.  Molecules in a gas _____

    _____

# Picture Perfect Liquids

Decide which of the following items are liquids.  Color only the ones that are liquid.  Cut out and glue them to your 'Picture Perfect Liquids' page.

# Picture Perfect Liquids

**Matter and Materials** - Skill: The students will discover, through experimentation, the interactions between liquids, and between liquids and solids.

# Mixing Liquids and Matter

## Part One

Mix the following and draw the results, using the correct colors on the chart.

You will need:

several clear plastic cups
red, blue and yellow food coloring
water

Drop five drops of blue food colouring into a half glass of water

Do the same with yellow food coloring.

Pour the yellow water into the blue water.

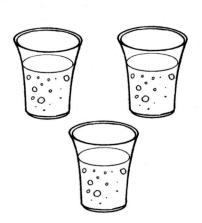

Do the same with yellow and red food coloring.

Now try again with blue and red.

Complete the chart below with pictures.

| Color Mixture | Result |
|---|---|
| Yellow and Blue | |
| Yellow and Red | |
| Blue and Red | |

Are you able to separate the colors? Why or why not?

______________________________________________

______________________________________________

# Mixing Liquids and Matter

## Part Two:

In this part of the activity you will need to add 59 ml (20 oz) of flour to 59 ml (20 oz) of water.

1. What happened when you combined the flour and water?

   _____

   _____

2. If you let your experiment dry, will the flour become soft again?  Try it and find out.

   _____

   _____

## Part Three:

In this part of the activity, you will need to pour 59 ml (20 oz) of vinegar into an empty pop bottle.  Add 14 ml (1/2 oz) of baking soda.

1. What happened when you added the baking soda?

   _____

   _____

2. What type of matter was produced?

   _____

   _____

3. What type of matter is the baking soda?

   _____

   _____

4. What type of matter is the vinegar?

   _____

   _____

# Comparing Liquids

This activity may be done as a whole class with different students carrying out the activities. As an alternative, students may draw pictures of the before and after aspects of the experiment.

In this activity, you will compare the properties of liquid materials.

## You will need:

water, ketchup, molasses (or another thick syrup), oil, desktop, paper towel, newspaper, plain white paper and a baking dish

## Directions:

1. Pour a small amount of each liquid onto the paper towel, newspaper, white paper, your desktop and into the baking pan.

2. On the following charts, record or draw what you see happening (example: it gets absorbed, it spreads quickly or slowly).

| Water | What Happened? |
|---|---|
| **Paper Towel** | |
| **Newspaper** | |
| **White Paper** | |
| **Desktop** | |
| **Baking Dish** | |

| Molasses | What Happened? |
|---|---|
| **Paper Towel** | |
| **Newspaper** | |
| **White Paper** | |
| **Desktop** | |
| **Baking Dish** | |

| Oil | What Happened? |
|---|---|
| **Paper Towel** | |
| **Newspaper** | |
| **White Paper** | |
| **Desktop** | |
| **Baking Dish** | |

| Ketchup | What Happened? |
|---|---|
| **Paper Towel** 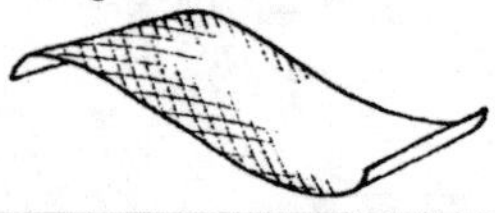 | |
| **Newspaper**  | |
| **White Paper**  | |
| **Desktop**  | |
| **Baking Dish**  | |

On the following chart, using your experiment results, record any similarities and differences you saw in your experiments.

| Liquids | Similarities | Differences |
|---|---|---|
| **Water and Oil** | | |
| **Water and Ketchup** | | |
| **Water and Molasses** | | |
| **Oil and Ketchup** | | |
| **Oil and Molasses** | | |
| **Ketchup and Molasses** | | |

# Do I Take Up Space?

This experiment may be done as a whole class or in small groups. In the following activity you will find out how solids and liquids take up space.

## You will need:

ice cubes, water, sand, flour, marbles, various liquids and several clear plastic cups

## Directions:

1. Fill half of your plastic cups with each of your solids and liquids.

2. Decide whether the material in each cup is a solid or a liquid.

3. Check carefully to see if all the space in the half of the cup is taken up with what you put in.

4. Record your results in the following chart.

| Material | Solid/Liquid | Took Up All of the Space | Left Some of the Space |
|----------|--------------|--------------------------|------------------------|
| Ice Cubes |  |  |  |
| Water |  |  |  |
| Sand |  |  |  |
| Marbles |  |  |  |
| Flour |  |  |  |
|  |  |  |  |

## Discussion Questions:

1. Was the solid or the liquid more likely to take up all the space?

2. Which solids took up all the space?

3. Which solids left spaces?

4. Why did some solids leave spaces and others didn't?

5. Why did the liquids take up all the space?

6. If you wanted to completely fill a bucket, would you be more likely to choose a liquid or a solid to do the job? Why?

# Magic Ice

The following is a teacher directed activity best performed by modeling the steps for young children.

In this activity, you will be turning a liquid into a solid and then back into a liquid. Sound impossible? Try this and find out!

## You will need:

any size wide-mouthed plastic container (yogurt or margarine containers work best), water, food coloring, a deep baking dish and a place to freeze the water.

## Directions:

1. Fill your container with water.

2. Add enough food coloring to get the color you want and mix together.

3. Place in a freezer for 24 hours.

4. When the water is frozen, remove from the container into a deep baking dish.

5. An extension of this activity is to stack ice and make colorful ice sculptures.

## Discussion Questions (Part One):

1. Is water a solid or a liquid?

2. What did you turn the water into?

3. Is that substance a solid or a liquid?

4. Why does water turn to ice in the winter?

## Next Step:

Now that you have made your object, leave it in your classroom for 24 hours.

## Discussion Questions (Part Two):

1. What did the solid become?

2. Is the new substance the same as when you first started the experiment?

3. Why does ice melt in the spring?

# Solids May Melt!

In the previous activity, you turned a liquid into a solid and then back into a liquid. In this activity, you will turn a solid into a liquid and then back into a solid.

## You will need:

small bits of different colored crayons, a small baking dish, tinfoil and a toaster oven

## Note:

A regular stove may be used for a large numbers of assignments. Use low heat to melt the crayon. Also, the baking dishes will be hot to the touch when they come out of the oven. Make sure there is a large, ventilated area where they may cool, out of reach.

## Directions:

1. Place a layer of tin foil in the baking dish.

2. Arrange your bits of crayons into a colorful pattern. Bake in a toaster oven until melted.

3. When the crayons have hardened, remove from the baking pan.

## Discussion Questions:

1. At the beginning of the experiment, are the crayons solids or liquids?

2. At the very end of the experiment, are the crayons solids or liquids?

3. What must have happened to the crayons in order for them to look like they do at the end?

4. When the crayons were melting, were they turning into a solid, liquid or gas?

5. Can you turn the crayons back to their original form? Why or why not?

# Make It Rain

In this activity, you will turn a liquid into a gas and then back into a liquid.

## Note:

Since you will be creating steam, and steam can leave a bad burn, it is suggested that the teacher perform the activity and that the students draw what they see happen.

**You Need:** a kettle full of water and a chilled plate.

## Directions:

1. Plug in the kettle until the steam begins to rise.

2. Hold the chilled plate over the steam. You may want to do this over some paper towel.

In the following space, draw a picture of what you saw happen.

## Discussion Questions:

1. Is the water in the kettle a solid, liquid or gas?

2. Is the steam a solid, liquid or gas?

3. What happened when the steam hit the plate?

# Picture Perfect Gases

Decide which of the following items are gases. Color only the ones that are gases. Cut them out and glue them to your 'Picture Perfect Gases' page.

# Picture Perfect Gases

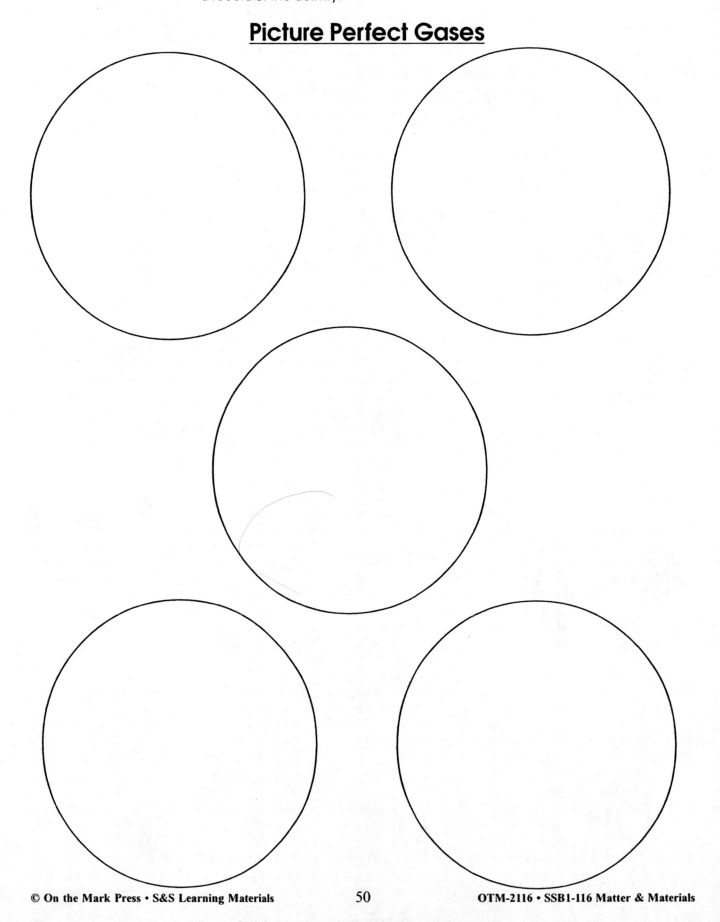

**Winter Gases**

In the winter, when the weather gets cold, you can see your breath outside.

This breath that you are blowing out is a 'gas'. When your warm breath meets the cold air, tiny water droplets form that allow you to see them.

Draw a winter picture of a time when you saw your breath.

# Colors Matter

**Color** the following picture using the color key below.

| | | |
|---|---|---|
| solids - **brown** | gases - **gray** | liquids - **blue** |

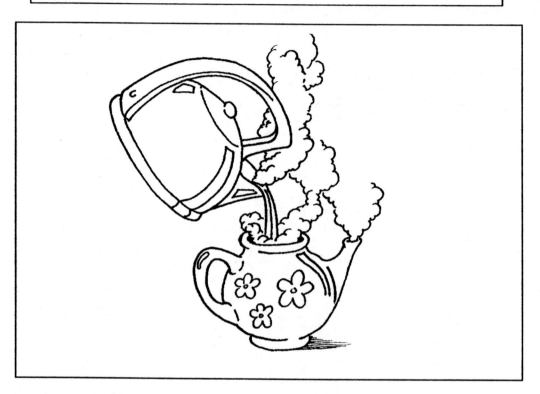

## Discussion Questions:

1. What type of matter is the tea pot? _____

2. What type of matter is the steam coming from the spout of the kettle? _____

3. What type of matter is coming from the kettle to the tea pot?

   _____

4. Now you know that a solid can hold things inside. Can a liquid hold things? Explain.

   _____

   _____

5. Can a gas hold anything? _____

# Make a Magazine

Using the knowledge that you have learned about solids, liquids, gases and materials, create a five page magazine highlighting these topics.

## Solids

Cut pictures from a magazine or draw pictures of at least **ten** different solids. You may want to highlight one as a special feature because it is a unique solid. For example, ice is special because it can turn into a liquid and a gas.

## Liquids

Cut pictures from a magazine or draw at least **ten** different liquids. You may want to highlight one as a special feature because it is a unique liquid. For example, water is special because it can turn into a solid and a gas.

## Gases

Cut pictures from a magazine or draw at least **three** different gases. You may want to highlight one as a special feature because it is a unique gas. For example, steam is special because it can turn into a liquid and a solid.

## Materials

Cut pictures from a magazine or draw at least **ten** different materials that can be used to make other things, For example, cotton is a solid material that can be made into clothing.

Be sure to make a cover for your magazine with a title and your name.

# Charge It!

In this activity, you will charge a balloon with static electricity.

## You will need:

a blown-up balloon, a wall and small pieces of tissue paper

## Directions (Part One):

1. Begin by holding your balloon up against the closest wall. What happens?

2. Now rub the balloon in your hair five to seven times and then hold it up against the closest wall. Let go of the balloon. What happens this time?

## Observations:

What you just saw was static electricity. Just as a battery charger charges a dead battery, your hair charged the balloon. Have you ever experienced static electricity in your life? Have you ever received a shock when you touched your friend after shuffling your feet on the carpet? Try it. That shock is static electricity. The shuffling of your feet on the carpet gives you a static electrical charge.

## Directions (Part Two):

1. With your balloon, try this experiment: Rub the balloon in your hair as you did before. Hold the balloon close to several small pieces of tissue paper.

2. What happens?

3. How many pieces of tissue paper did your balloon pick up?

4. Can you make the balloon pick up more?

5. What is the most number of pieces of tissue paper your balloon is able to pick up?

6. How far away can you hold the balloon and have it pick up tissue paper?

7. If you slide your hand on the balloon, will it still pick up tissue paper?

# How Strong Is a Static Electric Charge

In this activity, you will discover the strength of a static electric charge.

## You will need:

several small pieces of tissue paper, a plastic comb, a styrofoam cup, a balloon and a piece of nylon (stockings will do perfectly).

## Directions:

1. Rub certain materials together as suggested on the chart below.

2. Then see how many pieces of tissue paper they can pick up.

3. Record your results on the chart below.

4. Try each experiment twice.

| Materials Rubbed Together | Trial One | Trial Two |
|---|---|---|
| Balloon and Nylon | | |
| Styrofoam and Nylon | | |
| Plastic Comb and Nylon | | |

## Questions

1. Which combination picked up the most pieces of tissue paper?

2. Which combination picked up the least?

3. If you wanted to create a strong static electric charge, which would you choose?

# What Will Magnets Attract?

## You will need:

| | | |
|---|---|---|
| a wooden pencil | aluminum foil | bottle cap |
| plastic ruler | wire | penny |
| nickel | dime | quarter |
| dollar | pins | tacks |
| nail | eraser | cloth |
| paper clip | key | paper |
| tin can | pop can | comb |
| box | magnets | |

## Directions:

1. Put all the objects, except the magnets, in a big box.
2. Look at each object carefully.
3. Guess whether or not each object will be attracted to the magnet.
4. Then, with the magnet, try to pick up an object from the box.
5. If the magnet picks up the object, take it out of the box.
6. When you are finished complete the chart below by drawing pictures of each item or by printing its name.

| I discovered that....... | |
|---|---|
| These objects **were** attracted | These objects **were not** attracted |
| | |

# What things will a magnet work through?

## You will need:

| | | |
|---|---|---|
| magnets | plastic bag | paper clips |
| glass jar | piece of cloth | piece of nylon |
| paper plate | wooden ruler | piece of cardboard |
| elastic | | |

## Directions:

1. Look at each item in the box carefully.

2. Guess whether or not a magnet will be able to work through each item to attract a paper clip.

3. Next, wrap the cloth around the end of a magnet and fasten it with an elastic band.

4. Try to pick up a paper clip with the end of the magnet that is wrapped.

5. If the paper clip is attracted, put the cloth outside the box.

6. If the paper clip is not attracted, leave the cloth in the box.

7. Repeat using the other objects with the same magnet and the same paper clip.

8. When you are finished complete the chart below by drawing pictures of each item or by printing its name.

| I discovered that...... | |
|---|---|
| a magnet **will** work through these things | a magnet **will not** work through these things |
| | |

# Matter Quiz

Name: _____ Date: _____

Answer the following as completely as you can.

1. <u>Fill in the blank:</u>

a) Everything is made up of _____.

b) Matter can be broken into three smaller parts.

They are called _____, _____ and

_____ .

c) A liquid takes the _____ of its container.

d) Air is an example of a _____.

e) Your chair is an example of a _____.

2. <u>Matching:</u>

Draw a line from the words in column A with the correct words or

phrases in column B.

|  A  |  B  |
|  :---:  |  :---:  |
|  solid  |  water  |
|  matter  |  air  |
|  milk  |  gas  |
|  liquid  |  liquid  |
|  exhaust fumes  |  chair  |
|  gas  |  everything  |

# Matter Quiz

3. Listing

   List three objects beside the words below that are made from that material.

   Wood   1.   _____

           2.   _____

           3.   _____

   Plastic   1.   _____

           2.   _____

           3.   _____

4. Answer the following questions:

a) Why must the top of your desk be hard?

   _____

   _____

b) What will you create when you mix blue and yellow water?

   _____

   _____

5. Fill in the following chart:

| Materials Mixed | Will/Won't Mix |
|---|---|
| Cooking oil with water | |
| Dirt with water | |
| Sugar with warm water | |
| Pebbles with warm water | |

# Matter and Materials

Look for these material words in the word search.

| | | | | | |
|---|---|---|---|---|---|
| car | metal | smooth | plastic | window | flexible |
| dull | rough | rubber | soft | tree | inflexible |
| hard | shiny | wood | | | |

| | | | | | | | | | | | | | |
|---|---|---|---|---|---|---|---|---|---|---|---|---|---|
| e | l | b | i | x | e | l | f | n | i | e | d | d | d | o |
| c | i | t | s | a | l | p | r | u | b | b | e | r | k | g |
| e | u | t | i | m | e | g | q | i | x | e | h | r | a | c |
| n | x | r | e | w | o | d | n | i | w | e | y | f | t | h |
| g | r | t | d | s | p | o | g | s | o | n | r | u | n | j |
| r | a | c | m | j | x | o | t | k | i | y | i | n | b | k |
| l | l | u | d | t | s | w | h | h | s | w | d | v | r | y |
| s | y | u | g | i | g | f | s | g | s | h | p | l | h | i |
| g | c | x | r | q | z | m | s | u | e | v | e | k | v | m |
| u | j | i | j | v | m | t | i | o | e | g | i | m | p | k |
| l | w | j | d | m | w | x | d | r | f | h | o | n | a | q |
| v | b | t | f | y | b | p | z | n | a | t | x | g | r | o |

# Matter and Materials

Look for these matter words in the word search.

| air | liquid | solid | chair | matter |
|-----|--------|-------|-------|--------|
| taste | flexible | see | touch | gas |
| smell | water | hard | soft | |

| l | i | q | u | i | d | m | a | t | t | e | r |
|---|---|---|---|---|---|---|---|---|---|---|---|
| p | l | e | w | d | w | g | w | a | j | v | i |
| j | e | e | l | e | m | a | l | s | j | e | a |
| l | u | s | m | b | a | s | t | t | f | o | h |
| d | i | l | o | s | i | e | y | e | b | a | c |
| f | d | r | a | f | e | x | t | g | r | b | u |
| o | c | t | n | s | t | c | e | d | e | e | o |
| d | a | i | m | f | g | t | z | l | r | t | t |
| a | h | l | v | c | c | w | h | r | f | h | b |

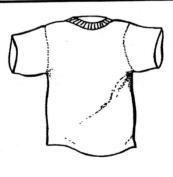

# Matter and Materials

## Answer Key

**Which Is It? (p. 26)**

Grocery Bag - plastic, flexible

Plastic Wrap - plastic, flexible

Tree - wood, hard

Pencil - wood, hard

Eraser - rubber, flexible

Tires - rubber, hard, flexible

Car - metal (steel), hard

T-shirt - cotton, flexible

Pencil Box - plastic, hard

Window - glass, hard

**Questions: (p. 27)**

1. Rubber and plastic are both hard and flexible   2. It can stretch to take in hard solids
3. The desk top is hard to support work materials   4. It won't tear the paper   5. It is flexible

**Will It float?  (p. 29)**

**Questions for Discussions**

1. There are air spaces in the ball.      2. It is denser than water, or the surface tension of the water wasn't strong enough to hold it up.      3. Answers will vary.  Examples: Air pockets will keep things light. The more water something displaces in relation to its weight, the more likely it will sink.

**More Matter (p. 37)**

1. touch, taste, smell, see, matter   2. three, solids, liquids, gases   3. too small to see without a microscope   4. pressed close together   5. move and flow   6. bounce off each other randomly and have large spaces between them

**Mixing Liquids and Matter**
**Part One: (p. 40)**

Yellow and Blue - green;   Yellow and red - orange;   Blue and Red - purple

**Part Two: (p. 41)**

1. It turned to a thick paste.   2. Answers will vary.

**Part Three: (p. 41)**

1. It bubbled and fizzed.   2. gas   3. solid   4. liquid

**Do I Take Up Space?**

**Discussion Questions: (p. 45)**

1. liquid   2. sand, flour   3. ice cubes, marbles   4. It depends on their size.
5. There is very little space between the molecules.   6. liquid - It always takes up all of the space.

## Magic Ice

### Discussion Questions: Part One (p. 46)
1. liquid   2. solid (ice)   3. solid   4. The temperature drops to freezing.

### Discussion Questions: Part Two (p. 46)
1. liquid (water)   2. Yes   3. The temperature warms above freezing.

## Solids May Melt

### Discussion Questions: (p. 47)
1. solids   2. solids   3. They had to melt into a liquid and mix together.   4. liquid
5. No. They cannot be separated.

## Make It Rain

### Discussion Questions: (p. 48)
1. liquid   2. gas   3. It turned to rain.

## Colors Matter

### Discussion Questions: (p. 52)
1. solid   2. gas   3. liquid   4. Yes, if it is thick enough   5. Yes, smells

## Charge It

### Discussion Questions: Part One (p. 54)

1. It falls to the ground.   2. It sticks to the wall.

### Discussion Questions: Part Two (p. 54)
2. It pulls the tissue paper to it.   3. to 7. Answers will vary.

## Matter Quiz (p. 58-59)

1. a) matter  b) solids, liquids, gases  c) shape  d) gas  e) solid
2. solid - chair;  matter - everything;   milk - liquid;  liquid - water;   exhaust fumes - gas
   gas - air
3. Answers will vary.
4. a) to support work materials   b) green water
5. Chart:
   Cooking oil with water - won't;   Dirt with water - will
   Sugar with warm water - will;   Pebbles with warm water - won't

## Materials Word Search

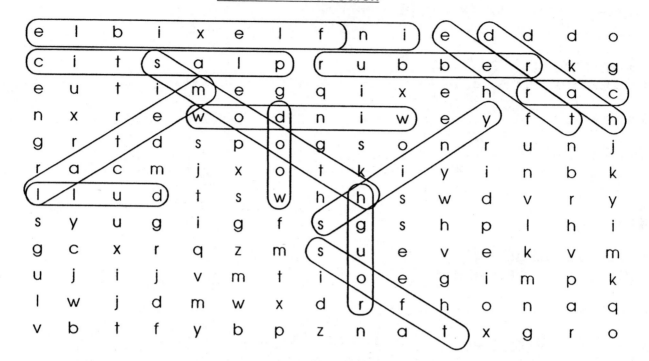

```
e  l  b  i  x  e  l  f  n  i  e  d  d  d  o
c  i  t  s  a  l  p  r  u  b  b  e  r  k  g
e  u  t  i  m  e  g  q  i  x  e  h  r  a  c
n  x  r  e  w  o  d  n  i  w  e  y  f  t  h
g  r  t  d  s  p  o  g  s  o  n  r  u  n  j
r  a  c  m  j  x  o  t  k  i  y  i  n  b  k
l  l  u  d  t  s  w  h  h  s  w  d  v  r  y
s  y  u  g  i  g  f  s  g  s  h  p  l  h  i
g  c  x  r  q  z  m  s  u  e  v  e  k  v  m
u  j  i  j  v  m  t  i  o  e  g  i  m  p  k
l  w  j  d  m  w  x  d  r  f  h  o  n  a  q
v  b  t  f  y  b  p  z  n  a  t  x  g  r  o
```

## Matter Word Search

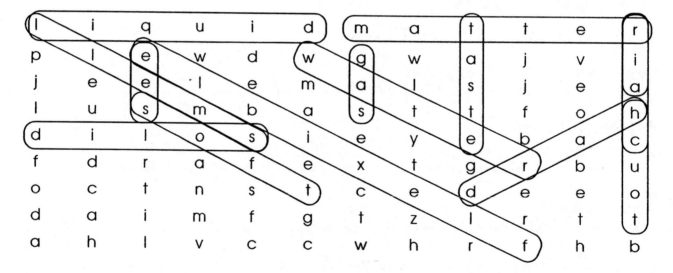

```
l  i  q  u  i  d        m  a  t  t  e  r
p  l  e  w  d        w  g  w  a  j  v  i
j  e  e  l  e        m  a  l  s  j  e  a
l  u  s  m  b        a  s  t  f  o  h
d  i  l  o  s  i        e  y  g  a  c
f  d  r  a  f  e        x  t  g  r  b  u
o  c  t  n  s  t        c  e  t  d  e  o
d  a  i  m  f  g        t  z  l  r  t
a  h  l  v  c  c        w  h  r  f  h  b
```

# Publication Listing

See Dealer or
www.sslearning.com
For Pricing
1-800-463-6367

| Code # | Title and Grade |
|---|---|
| SSC1-12 | A Time of Plenty Gr. 2 |
| SSN1-92 | Abel's Island NS 4-6 |
| SSF1-16 | Aboriginal Peoples of Canada Gr. 7-8 |
| SSK1-31 | Addition & Subtraction Drills Gr. 1-3 |
| SSK1-28 | Addition Drills Gr. 1-3 |
| SSY1-04 | Addition Gr. 1-3 |
| SSN1-174 | Adv. of Huckle Berry Finn NS 7-8 |
| SSB1-63 | African Animals Gr 4-6 |
| SSB1-29 | All About Bears Gr. 1-2 |
| SSF1-08 | All About Boats Gr. 2-3 |
| SSJ1-02 | All About Canada Gr. 2 |
| SSB1-54 | All About Cattle Gr. 4-6 |
| SSN1-10 | All About Colours Gr. P-1 |
| SSB1-93 | All About Dinosaurs Gr. 2 |
| SSN1-14 | All About Dragons Gr. 3-5 |
| SSB1-07 | All About Elephants Gr. 3-4 |
| SSB1-68 | All About Fish Gr. 4-6 |
| SSN1-39 | All About Giants Gr. 2-3 |
| SSH1-15 | All About Jobs Gr. 1-3 |
| SSH1-05 | All About Me Gr. 1 |
| SSA1-02 | All About Mexico Gr. 4-6 |
| SSR1-28 | All About Nouns Gr. 5-7 |
| SSF1-09 | All About Planes Gr. 2-3 |
| SSB1-33 | All About Plants Gr. 2-3 |
| SSR1-29 | All About Pronouns Gr. 5-7 |
| SSB1-12 | All About Rabbits Gr. 2-3 |
| SSB1-58 | All About Spiders Gr. 4-6 |
| SSA1-03 | All About the Desert Gr. 4-6 |
| SSA1-04 | All About the Ocean Gr. 5-7 |
| SSZ1-01 | All About the Olympics Gr. 2-4 |
| SSB1-49 | All About the Sea Gr. 4-6 |
| SSK1-06 | All About Time Gr. 4-6 |
| SSF1-07 | All About Trains Gr. 2-3 |
| SSH1-18 | All About Transportation Gr. 2 |
| SSB1-01 | All About Trees Gr. 4-6 |
| SSB1-61 | All About Weather Gr. 7-8 |
| SSB1-06 | All About Whales Gr. 3-4 |
| SSPC-26 | All Kinds of Clocks B/W Pictures |
| SSB1-110 | All Kinds of Structures Gr. 1 |
| SSH1-19 | All Kinds of Vehicles Gr. 3 |
| SSF1-01 | Amazing Aztecs Gr. 4-6 |
| SSB1-92 | Amazing Earthworms Gr. 2-3 |
| SSJ1-50 | Amazing Facts in Cdn History Gr. 4-6 |
| SSB1-32 | Amazing Insects Gr. 4-6 |
| SSN1-132 | Amelia Bedelia–Camping NS 1-3 |
| SSN1-68 | Amelia Bedelia NS 1-3 |
| SSN1-155 | Amelia Bedelia-Surprise Shower NS 1-3 |
| SSA1-13 | America The Beautiful Gr. 4-6 |
| SSN1-57 | Amish Adventure NS 7-8 |
| SSF1-02 | Ancient China Gr. 4-6 |
| SSF1-18 | Ancient Egypt Gr. 4-6 |
| SSF1-21 | Ancient Greece Gr. 4-6 |
| SSF1-19 | Ancient Rome Gr. 4-6 |
| SSQ1-06 | Animal Town – Big Book Pkg 1-3 |
| SSQ1-02 | Animals Prepare Winter- Big Book Pkg 1-3 |
| SSN1-150 | Animorphs the Invasion NS 4-6 |
| SSN1-53 | Anne of Green Gables NS 7-8 |
| SSB1-40 | Apple Celebration Gr. 4-6 |
| SSB1-04 | Apple Mania Gr. 2-3 |
| SSB1-38 | Apples are the Greatest Gr. P-K |
| SSB1-59 | Arctic Animals Gr. 4-6 |
| SSN1-162 | Arnold Lobel Author Study Gr. 2-3 |
| SSPC-22 | Australia B/W Pictures |
| SSA1-05 | Australia Gr. 5-8 |
| SSM1-03 | Autumn in the Woodlot Gr. 2-3 |
| SSM1-08 | Autumn Wonders Gr. 1 |
| SSN1-41 | Baby Sister for Frances NS 1-3 |
| SSPC-19 | Back to School B/W Pictures |
| SSC1-33 | Back to School Gr. 2-3 |
| SSN1-224 | Banner in the Sky NS 7-8 |
| SSN1-36 | Bargain for Frances NS 1-3 |
| SSB1-82 | Bats Gr. 4-6 |
| SSN1-71 | BB – Drug Free Zone NS Gr. 1-3 |
| SSN1-88 | BB – In the Freaky House NS 1-3 |
| SSN1-78 | BB – Media Madness NS 1-3 |
| SSN1-69 | BB – Wheelchair Commando NS 1-3 |
| SSN1-119 | Be a Perfect Person-3 Days NS 4-6 |
| SSC1-15 | Be My Valentine Gr. 1 |
| SSD1-01 | Be Safe Not Sorry Gr. P-1 |

| Code # | Title and Grade |
|---|---|
| SSN1-09 | Bear Tales Gr. 2-4 |
| SSB1-28 | Bears Gr. 4-6 |
| SSN1-202 | Bears in Literature Gr. 1-3 |
| SSN1-40 | Beatrix Potter Gr. 2-4 |
| SSN1-129 | Beatrix Potter: Activity Biography 2-4 |
| SSB1-47 | Beautiful Bugs Gr. 1 |
| SSB1-21 | Beavers Gr. 3-5 |
| SSN1-257 | Because of Winn-Dixie NS Gr. 4-6 |
| SSR1-53 | Beginning Manuscript Gr. Pk-2 |
| SSR1-54 | Beginning Cursive Gr. 2-4 |
| SSN1-33 | Bedtime for Frances NS 1-3 |
| SSN1-114 | Best Christmas Pageant Ever NS 4-6 |
| SSN1-32 | Best Friends for Frances NS 1-3 |
| SSB1-39 | Best Friends Pets Gr. P-K |
| SSN1-185 | BFG NS Gr. 4-6 |
| SSN1-35 | Birthday for Frances NS Gr. 1-3 |
| SSN1-107 | Borrowers NS Gr. 4-6 |
| SSC1-16 | Bouquet of Valentines Gr. 2 |
| SSN1-29 | Bread & Jam for Frances NS 1-3 |
| SSN1-63 | Bridge to Terabithia NS Gr. 4-6 |
| SSY1-24 | BTS Numeración Gr. 1-3 |
| SSY1-25 | BTS Adición Gr. 1-3 |
| SSY1-26 | BTS Sustracción Gr. 1-3 |
| SSY1-27 | BTS Fonética Gr. 1-3 |
| SSY1-28 | BTS Leer para Entender Gr. 1-3 |
| SSY1-29 | BTS Uso de las Mayúsculas y Reglas de Puntuación Gr. 1-3 |
| SSY1-30 | BTS Composición de Oraciones Gr. 1-3 |
| SSY1-31 | BTS Composici13n de Historias Gr. 1-3 |
| SSN1-256 | Bud, Not Buddy NS Gr. 4-6 |
| SSB1-31 | Bugs, Bugs & More Bugs Gr. 2-3 |
| SSR1-07 | Building Word Families L.V. 1-2 |
| SSR1-05 | Building Word Families S.V. 1-2 |
| SSN1-204 | Bunnicula NS Gr. 4-6 |
| SSB1-80 | Butterflies & Caterpillars Gr. 1-2 |
| SSN1-164 | Call It Courage NS Gr. 7-8 |
| SSN1-67 | Call of the Wild NS Gr. 7-8 |
| SSJ1-41 | Canada & It's Trading Partners 6-8 |
| SSPC-28 | Canada B/W Pictures |
| SSN1-173 | Canada Geese Quilt NS Gr. 4-6 |
| SSJ1-01 | Canada Gr. 1 |
| SSJ1-33 | Canada's Capital Cities Gr. 4-6 |
| SSJ1-43 | Canada's Confederation Gr. 7-8 |
| SSF1-04 | Canada's First Nations Gr. 7-8 |
| SSJ1-51 | Canada's Landmarks Gr. 1-3 |
| SSJ1-48 | Canada's Landmarks Gr. 4-6 |
| SSJ1-42 | Canada's Traditions & Celeb. Gr. 1-3 |
| SSB1-45 | Canadian Animals Gr. 1-2 |
| SSJ1-37 | Canadian Arctic Inuit Gr. 2-3 |
| SSJ1-53 | Canadian Black History Gr. 4-8 |
| SSJ1-57 | Canadian Comprehension Gr. 1-2 |
| SSJ1-58 | Canadian Comprehension Gr. 3-4 |
| SSJ1-59 | Canadian Comprehension Gr. 5-6 |
| SSJ1-46 | Canadian Industries Gr. 4-6 |
| SSK1-12 | Canadian Problem Solving Gr. 4-6 |
| SSJ1-38 | Canadian Provinces & Terr. Gr. 4-6 |
| SSY1-07 | Capitalization & Punctuation Gr. 1-3 |
| SSN1-198 | Captain Courageous NS Gr. 7-8 |
| SSK1-11 | Cars Problem Solving Gr. 3-4 |
| SSN1-154 | Castle in the Attic NS Gr. 4-6 |
| SSF1-31 | Castles & Kings Gr. 4-6 |
| SSN1-144 | Cat Ate My Gymsuit NS Gr. 4-6 |
| SSPC-38 | Cats B/W Pictures |
| SSB1-50 | Cats – Domestic & Wild Gr. 4-6 |
| SSN1-34 | Cats in Literature Gr. 3-6 |
| SSN1-212 | Cay NS Gr. 7-8 |
| SSM1-09 | Celebrate Autumn Gr. 4-6 |
| SSC1-39 | Celebrate Christmas Gr. 4-6 |
| SSC1-31 | Celebrate Easter Gr. 4-6 |
| SSC1-23 | Celebrate Shamrock Day Gr. 2 |
| SSM1-11 | Celebrate Spring Gr. 4-6 |
| SSC1-13 | Celebrate Thanksgiving R. 3-4 |
| SSM1-06 | Celebrate Winter Gr. 4-6 |
| SSB1-107 | Cells, Tissues & Organs Gr. 7-8 |
| SSB1-101 | Characteristics of Flight Gr. 4-6 |
| SSN1-66 | Charlie & Chocolate Factory NS 4-6 |
| SSN1-23 | Charlotte's Web NS Gr. 4-6 |
| SSB1-37 | Chicks N'Ducks Gr. 2-4 |
| SSA1-09 | China Today Gr. 5-8 |
| SSN1-70 | Chocolate Fever NS Gr. 4-6 |
| SSN1-241 | Chocolate Touch NS Gr. 4-6 |
| SSC1-38 | Christmas Around the World Gr. 4-6 |
| SSPC-42 | Christmas B/W Pictures |
| SST1-08A | Christmas Gr. JK/SK |
| SST1-08B | Christmas Gr. 1 |
| SST1-08C | Christmas Gr. 2-3 |
| SSC1-04 | Christmas Magic Gr. 1 |
| SSC1-03 | Christmas Tales Gr. 2-3 |
| SSG1-06 | Cinematography Gr. 5-8 |
| SSPC-13 | Circus B/W Pictures |

| Code # | Title and Grade |
|---|---|
| SSF1-03 | Circus Magic Gr. 3-4 |
| SSJ1-52 | Citizenship/Immigration Gr. 4-8 |
| SSN1-104 | Classical Poetry Gr. 7-12 |
| SSN1-227 | Color Gr. 1-3 |
| SSN1-203 | Colour Gr. 1-3 |
| SSN1-135 | Come Back Amelia Bedelia NS 1-3 |
| SSH1-11 | Community Helpers Gr. 1-3 |
| SSK1-02 | Concept Cards & Activities Gr. P-1 |
| SSN1-183 | Copper Sunrise NS Gr. 7-8 |
| SSN1-86 | Corduroy & Pocket Corduroy NS 1-3 |
| SSN1-124 | Could Dracula Live in Wood NS 4-6 |
| SSN1-148 | Cowboy's Don't Cry NS Gr. 7-8 |
| SSR1-01 | Creativity with Food Gr. 4-8 |
| SSB1-34 | Creatures of the Sea Gr. 2-4 |
| SSN1-208 | Curse of the Viking Grave NS 7-8 |
| SSN1-134 | Danny Champion of World NS 4-6 |
| SSN1-98 | Danny's Run NS Gr. 7-8 |
| SSK1-21 | Data Management Gr. 4-6 |
| SSB1-53 | Dealing with Dinosaurs Gr. 4-6 |
| SSN1-178 | Dear Mr. Henshaw NS Gr. 4-6 |
| SSB1-22 | Deer Gr. 3-5 |
| SSPC-20 | Desert B/W Pictures |
| SSJ1-40 | Development of Western Canada 7-8 |
| SSA1-16 | Development of Manufacturing 7-9 |
| SSN1-105 | Dicken's Christmas NS Gr. 7-8 |
| SSN1-62 | Different Dragons NS Gr. 4-6 |
| SSPC-21 | Dinosaurs B/W Pictures |
| SSB1-16 | Dinosaurs Gr. 1 |
| SST1-02A | Dinosaurs Gr. JK/SK |
| SST1-02B | Dinosaurs Gr. 1 |
| SST1-02 C | Dinosaurs Gr. 2-3 |
| SSN1-175 | Dinosaurs in Literature Gr. 1-3 |
| SSJ1-26 | Discover Nova Scotia Gr. 5-7 |
| SSJ1-36 | Discover Nunavut Territory Gr. 5-7 |
| SSJ1-25 | Discover Ontario Gr. 5-7 |
| SSJ1-24 | Discover PEI Gr. 5-7 |
| SSJ1-22 | Discover Québec Gr. 5-7 |
| SSL1-01 | Discovering the Library Gr. 2-3 |
| SSB1-106 | Diversity of Living Things Gr. 4-6 |
| SSK1-27 | Division Drills Gr. 4-6 |
| SSB1-30 | Dogs – Wild & Tame Gr. 4-6 |
| SSPC-31 | Dogs B/W Pictures |
| SSN1-196 | Dog's Don't Tell Jokes NS Gr. 4-6 |
| SSN1-182 | Door in the Wall NS Gr. 4-6 |
| SSB1-87 | Down by the Sea Gr. 1-3 |
| SSN1-189 | Dr. Jeckyll & Mr. Hyde NS Gr. 4-6 |
| SSG1-07 | Dragon Trivia Gr. P-8 |
| SSN1-102 | Dragon's Egg NS Gr. 4-6 |
| SSN1-16 | Dragons in Literature Gr. 3-6 |
| SSC1-06 | Early Christmas Gr. 3-5 |
| SSB1-109 | Earth's Crust Gr. 6-8 |
| SSC1-21 | Easter Adventures Gr. 3-4 |
| SSC1-17 | Easter Delights Gr. P-K |
| SSC1-19 | Easter Surprises Gr. 1 |
| SSPC-12 | Egypt B/W Pictures |
| SSN1-255 | Egypt Game NS Gr. 4-6 |
| SSF1-28 | Egyptians Today & Yesterday Gr. 2-3 |
| SSJ1-49 | Elections in Canada Gr. 4-8 |
| SSB1-108 | Electricity Gr. 4-6 |
| SSN1-02 | Elves & the Shoemaker NS Gr. 1-3 |
| SSH1-14 | Emotions Gr. P-2 |
| SSB1-85 | Energy Gr. 4-6 |
| SSN1-108 | English Language Gr. 10-12 |
| SSN1-156 | Enjoying Eric Wilson Series Gr. 5-7 |
| SSB1-64 | Environment Gr. 4-6 |
| SSR1-12 | ESL Teaching Ideas Gr. K-8 |
| SSN1-258 | Esperanza Rising NS Gr. 4-6 |
| SSR1-22 | Exercises in Grammar Gr. 6 |
| SSR1-23 | Exercises in Grammar Gr. 7 |
| SSR1-24 | Exercises in Grammar Gr. 8 |
| SSF1-20 | Exploration Gr. 4-6 |
| SSF1-15 | Explorers & Mapmakers of Can. 7-8 |
| SSJ1-54 | Exploring Canada Gr. 1-3 |
| SSJ1-56 | Exploring Canada Gr. 1-6 |
| SSJ1-55 | Exploring Canada Gr. 4-6 |
| SSH1-20 | Exploring My School & Community 1 |
| SSPC-39 | Fables B/W Pictures |
| SSN1-15 | Fables Gr. 4-6 |
| SSN1-04 | Fairy Tale Magic Gr. 3-5 |
| SSPC-11 | Fairy Tales B/W Pictures |
| SSN1-11 | Fairy Tales Gr. 1-2 |
| SSN1-199 | Family Under the Bridge NS 4-6 |
| SSPC-41 | Famous Canadians B/W Pictures |
| SSJ1-12 | Famous Canadians Gr. 4-8 |
| SSN1-210 | Fantastic Mr. Fox NS Gr. 4-6 |
| SSB1-36 | Fantastic Plants Gr. 4-6 |
| SSPC-04 | Farm Animals B/W Pictures |
| SSB1-15 | Farm Animals Gr. 1-2 |
| SST1-03A | Farm Gr. JK/SK |
| SST1-03B | Farm Gr. 1 |
| SST1-03C | Farm Gr. 2-3 |
| SSJ1-05 | Farming Community Gr. 3-4 |

| Code # | Title and Grade |
|---|---|
| SSB1-44 | Farmyard Friends Gr. P-K |
| SSJ1-45 | Fathers of Confederation Gr. 4-8 |
| SSB1-19 | Feathered Friends Gr. 4-6 |
| SST1-05A | February Gr. JK/SK |
| SST1-05B | February Gr. 1 |
| SST1-05C | February Gr. 2-3 |
| SSN1-03 | Festival of Fairytales Gr. 3-5 |
| SSC1-46 | Festivals Around the World Gr. 2-3 |
| SSN1-168 | First 100 Sight Words Gr. 1 |
| SSC1-32 | First Days at School Gr. 1 |
| SSJ1-06 | Fishing Community Gr. 3-4 |
| SSN1-170 | Flowers for Algernon NS Gr. 7-8 |
| SSN1-128 | Fly Away Home NS Gr. 4-6 |
| SSD1-05 | Food: Fact, Fun & Fiction Gr. 1-3 |
| SSD1-06 | Food: Nutrition & Invention Gr. 4-6 |
| SSB1-118 | Force and Motion Gr. 1-3 |
| SSB1-119 | Force and Motion Gr. 4-6 |
| SSB1-25 | Foxes Gr. 3-5 |
| SSN1-172 | Freckle Juice NS Gr. 1-3 |
| SSB1-43 | Friendly Frogs Gr. 1 |
| SSN1-260 | Frindle Gr. 4-6 |
| SSB1-89 | Fruits & Seeds Gr. 4-6 |
| SSN1-137 | Fudge-a-Mania NS Gr. 4-6 |
| SSB1-14 | Fun on the Farm Gr. 3-4 |
| SSR1-49 | Fun with Phonics Gr. 1-3 |
| SSPC-06 | Garden Flowers B/W Pictures |
| SSK1-03 | Geometric Shapes Gr. 2-5 |
| SSC1-18 | Get the Rabbit Habit Gr. 1-2 |
| SSN1-209 | Giver, The NS Gr. 7-8 |
| SSN1-190 | Go Jump in the Pool NS Gr. 4-6 |
| SSG1-03 | Goal Setting Gr. 6-8 |
| SSG1-08 | Gr. 3 Test – Parent Guide |
| SSG1-99 | Gr. 3 Test – Teacher Guide |
| SSG1-09 | Gr. 6 Language Test–Parent Guide |
| SSG1-97 | Gr. 6 Language Test–Teacher Guide |
| SSG1-10 | Gr. 6 Math Test – Parent Guide |
| SSG1-96 | Gr. 6 Math Test – Teacher Guide |
| SSG1-98 | Gr. 6 Math/Lang. Test–Teacher Guide |
| SSK1-14 | Graph for all Seasons Gr. 1-3 |
| SSN1-117 | Great Brain NS Gr. 4-6 |
| SSN1-90 | Great Expectations NS Gr. 7-8 |
| SSN1-169 | Great Gilly Hopkins NS Gr. 4-6 |
| SSN1-197 | Great Science Fair Disaster NS 4-6 |
| SSN1-138 | Greek Mythology Gr. 7-8 |
| SSN1-113 | Green Gables Detectives NS 4-6 |
| SSC1-26 | Groundhog Celebration Gr. 2 |
| SSC1-25 | Groundhog Day Gr. 1 |
| SSB1-113 | Growth & Change in Animals Gr. 2-3 |
| SSB1-114 | Growth & Change in Plants Gr. 2-3 |
| SSB1-48 | Guinea Pigs & Friends Gr. 3-5 |
| SSB1-104 | Habitats Gr. 4-6 |
| SSPC-18 | Halloween B/W Pictures |
| SST1-04A | Halloween Gr. JK/SK |
| SST1-04B | Halloween Gr. 1 |
| SST1-04C | Halloween Gr. 2-3 |
| SSC1-10 | Halloween Gr. 4-6 |
| SSC1-08 | Halloween Happiness Gr. 1 |
| SSC1-29 | Halloween Spirits Gr. P-K |
| SSC1-42 | Happy Valentines Day Gr. 3 |
| SSN1-205 | Harper Moon NS Gr. 7-8 |
| SSN1-123 | Harriet the Spy NS Gr. 4-6 |
| SSC1-11 | Harvest Time Wonders Gr. 1 |
| SSN1-136 | Hatchet NS Gr. 7-8 |
| SSC1-09 | Haunting Halloween Gr. 2-3 |
| SSN1-91 | Hawk & Stretch NS Gr. 4-6 |
| SSC1-30 | Hearts & Flowers Gr. P-K |
| SSN1-22 | Heidi NS Gr. 4-6 |
| SSN1-120 | Help I'm Trapped in My NS 4-6 |
| SSN1-24 | Henry & the Clubhouse NS 4-6 |
| SSN1-184 | Hobbit NS Gr. 7-8 |
| SSN1-122 | Hoboken Chicken Emerg. NS 4-6 |
| SSN1-250 | Holes NS Gr. 4-6 |
| SSN1-116 | How Can a Frozen Detective NS 4-6 |
| SSN1-89 | How Can I be a Detective if I NS 4-6 |
| SSN1-96 | How Come the Best Clues... NS 4-6 |
| SSN1-133 | How To Eat Fried Worms NS 4-6 |
| SSR1-48 | How To Give a Presentation Gr. 4-6 |
| SSN1-125 | How To Teach Writing Through 7-9 |
| SSR1-10 | How To Write a Composition 6-10 |
| SSR1-09 | How To Write a Paragraph 5-10 |
| SSR1-08 | How To Write an Essay Gr. 7-12 |
| SSR1-03 | How To Write Poetry & Stories 4-6 |
| SSD1-07 | Human Body Gr. 2-4 |
| SSD1-02 | Human Body Gr. 4-6 |
| SSN1-25 | I Want to Go Home NS Gr. 4-6 |
| SSH1-06 | I'm Important Gr. 2-3 |
| SSH1-07 | I'm Unique Gr. 4-6 |
| SSF1-05 | In Days of Yore Gr. 4-6 |
| SSF1-06 | In Pioneer Days Gr. 2-4 |
| SSM1-10 | In the Wintertime Gr. 2 |
| SSB1-41 | Incredible Dinosaurs Gr. P-1 |
| SSN1-177 | Incredible Journey NS Gr. 4-6 |

# Publication Listing

| Code # | Title and Grade |
|---|---|
| SSN1-100 | Indian in the Cupboard NS Gr. 4-6 |
| SSPC-05 | Insects B/W Pictures |
| SSPC-10 | Inuit B/W Pictures |
| SSJ1-10 | Inuit Community Gr. 3-4 |
| SSN1-85 | Ira Sleeps Over NS Gr. 1-3 |
| SSN1-93 | Iron Man NS Gr. 4-6 |
| SSN1-193 | Island of the Blue Dolphins NS 4-6 |
| SSB1-11 | It's a Dogs World Gr. 2-3 |
| SSM1-05 | It's a Marshmallow World Gr. 3 |
| SSK1-05 | It's About Time Gr. 2-4 |
| SSC1-41 | It's Christmas Time Gr. 3 |
| SSH1-04 | It's Circus Time Gr. 1 |
| SSC1-43 | It's Groundhog Day Gr. 3 |
| SSB1-75 | It's Maple Syrup Time Gr. 2-4 |
| SSC1-40 | It's Trick or Treat Time Gr. 2 |
| SSN1-65 | James & The Giant Peach NS 4-6 |
| SSN1-106 | Jane Eyre NS Gr. 7-8 |
| SSPC-25 | Japan B/W Pictures |
| SSA1-06 | Japan Gr. 5-8 |
| SSC1-05 | Joy of Christmas Gr. 2 |
| SSN1-161 | Julie of the Wolves NS Gr. 7-8 |
| SSB1-81 | Jungles Gr. 2-3 |
| SSE1-02 | Junior Music for Fall Gr. 4-6 |
| SSE1-05 | Junior Music for Spring Gr. 4-6 |
| SSE1-06 | Junior Music for Winter Gr. 4-6 |
| SSN1-151 | Kate NS Gr. 4-6 |
| SSN1-95 | Kidnapped in the Yukon NS Gr. 4-6 |
| SSN1-140 | Kids at Bailey School Gr. 2-4 |
| SSN1-176 | King of the Wind NS Gr. 4-6 |
| SSF1-29 | Klondike Gold Rush Gr. 4-6 |
| SSF1-33 | Labour Movement in Canada Gr. 7-8 |
| SSN1-152 | Lamplighter NS Gr. 4-6 |
| SSB1-98 | Learning About Dinosaurs Gr. 3 |
| SSN1-38 | Learning About Giants Gr. 4-6 |
| SSK1-22 | Learning About Measurement Gr. 1-3 |
| SSB1-46 | Learning About Mice Gr. 3-5 |
| SSK1-09 | Learning About Money CDN Gr. 1-3 |
| SSK1-19 | Learning About Money USA Gr. 1-3 |
| SSK1-23 | Learning About Numbers Gr. 1-3 |
| SSB1-69 | Learning About Rocks & Soils Gr. 2-3 |
| SSK1-08 | Learning About Shapes Gr. 1-3 |
| SSB1-100 | Learning About Simple Machines 1-3 |
| SSK1-04 | Learning About the Calendar Gr. 2-3 |
| SSK1-10 | Learning About Time Gr. 1-3 |
| SSH1-17 | Learning About Transportation Gr. 1 |
| SSB1-02 | Leaves Gr. 2-3 |
| SSN1-50 | Legends Gr. 4-6 |
| SSC1-27 | Lest We Forget Gr. 4-6 |
| SSJ1-13 | Let's Look at Canada Gr. 4-6 |
| SSJ1-16 | Let's Visit Alberta Gr. 2-4 |
| SSJ1-15 | Let's Visit British Columbia Gr. 2-4 |
| SSJ1-03 | Let's Visit Canada Gr. 3 |
| SSJ1-18 | Let's Visit Manitoba Gr. 2-4 |
| SSJ1-21 | Let's Visit New Brunswick Gr. 2-4 |
| SSJ1-27 | Let's Visit NFLD & Labrador Gr. 2-4 |
| SSJ1-30 | Let's Visit North West Terr. Gr. 2-4 |
| SSJ1-20 | Let's Visit Nova Scotia Gr. 2-4 |
| SSJ1-34 | Let's Visit Nunavut Gr. 2-4 |
| SSJ1-17 | Let's Visit Ontario Gr. 2-4 |
| SSQ1-08 | Let's Visit Ottawa Big Book Pkg 1-3 |
| SSJ1-19 | Let's Visit PEI Gr. 2-4 |
| SSJ1-31 | Let's Visit Québec Gr. 2-4 |
| SSJ1-14 | Let's Visit Saskatchewan Gr. 2-4 |
| SSJ1-28 | Let's Visit Yukon Gr. 2-4 |
| SSN1-130 | Life & Adv. of Santa Claus NS 7-8 |
| SSB1-10 | Life in a Pond Gr. 3-4 |
| SSF1-30 | Life in the Middle Ages Gr. 7-8 |
| SSB1-103 | Light & Sound Gr. 4-6 |
| SSN1-219 | Light in the Forest NS Gr. 7-8 |
| SSN1-121 | Light on Hogback Hill NS Gr. 4-6 |
| SSN1-46 | Lion, Witch & the Wardrobe NS 4-6 |
| SSR1-51 | Literature Response Forms Gr. 1-3 |
| SSR1-52 | Literature Response Forms Gr. 4-6 |
| SSN1-28 | Little House Big Woods NS 4-6 |
| SSN1-233 | Little House on the Prairie NS 4-6 |
| SSN1-111 | Little Women NS Gr. 7-8 |
| SSN1-115 | Live from the Fifth Grade NS 4-6 |
| SSN1-141 | Look Through My Window NS 4-6 |
| SSN1-112 | Look! Visual Discrimination Gr. P-1 |
| SSN1-61 | Lost & Found NS Gr. 4-6 |
| SSN1-109 | Lost in the Barrens NS Gr. 7-8 |
| SSJ1-08 | Lumbering Community Gr. 3-4 |
| SSN1-167 | Magic School Bus Gr. 1-3 |
| SSN1-247 | Magic Treehouse Gr. 1-3 |
| SSB1-78 | Magnets Gr. 3-5 |
| SSD1-03 | Making Sense of Our Senses K-1 |
| SSN1-146 | Mama's Going to Buy You a NS 4-6 |
| SSB1-94 | Mammals Gr. 1 |
| SSB1-95 | Mammals Gr. 2 |
| SSB1-96 | Mammals Gr. 3 |
| SSB1-97 | Mammals Gr. 5-6 |

| Code # | Title and Grade |
|---|---|
| SSN1-160 | Maniac Magee NS Gr. 4-6 |
| SSA1-19 | Mapping Activities & Outlines! 4-8 |
| SSA1-17 | Mapping Skills Gr. 1-3 |
| SSA1-07 | Mapping Skills Gr. 4-6 |
| SST1-10A | March Gr. JK/SK |
| SST1-10B | March Gr. 1 |
| SST1-10C | March Gr. 2-3 |
| SSB1-57 | Marvellous Marsupials Gr. 4-6 |
| SSK1-01 | Math Signs & Symbols Gr. 1-3 |
| SSB1-116 | Matter & Materials Gr. 1-3 |
| SSB1-117 | Matter & Materials Gr. 4-6 |
| SSH1-03 | Me, I'm Special! Gr. P-1 |
| SSK1-16 | Measurement Gr. 4-8 |
| SSC1-02 | Medieval Christmas Gr. 4-6 |
| SSPC-09 | Medieval Life B/W Pictures |
| SSC1-07 | Merry Christmas Gr. P-K |
| SSK1-15 | Metric Measurement Gr. 4-8 |
| SSN1-13 | Mice in Literature Gr. 3-5 |
| SSB1-70 | Microscopy Gr. 4-6 |
| SSN1-180 | Midnight Fox NS Gr. 4-6 |
| SSN1-243 | Midwife's Apprentice NS Gr. 4-6 |
| SSJ1-07 | Mining Community Gr. 3-4 |
| SSK1-17 | Money Talks – Cdn Gr. 3-6 |
| SSK1-18 | Money Talks – USA Gr. 3-6 |
| SSB1-56 | Monkeys & Apes Gr. 4-6 |
| SSN1-43 | Monkeys in Literature Gr. 2-4 |
| SSN1-54 | Monster Mania Gr. 4-6 |
| SSN1-97 | Mouse & the Motorcycle NS 4-6 |
| SSN1-94 | Mr. Poppers Penguins NS Gr. 4-6 |
| SSN1-201 | Mrs. Frisby & Rats NS Gr. 4-6 |
| SSR1-13 | Milti-Level Spelling Program Gr. 3-6 |
| SSR1-26 | Multi-Level Spelling USA Gr. 3-6 |
| SSK1-31 | Addition & Subtraction Drills 1-3 |
| SSK1-32 | Multiplication & Division Drills 4-6 |
| SSK1-30 | Multiplication Drills Gr. 4-6 |
| SSA1-14 | My Country! The USA! Gr. 2-4 |
| SSN1-186 | My Side of the Mountain NS 7-8 |
| SSN1-58 | Mysteries, Monsters & Magic Gr. 6-8 |
| SSN1-37 | Mystery at Blackrock Island NS 7-8 |
| SSN1-80 | Mystery House NS 4-6 |
| SSN1-157 | Nate the Great & Sticky Case NS 1-3 |
| SSF1-23 | Native People of North America 4-6 |
| SSF1-25 | New France Part 1 Gr. 7-8 |
| SSF1-27 | New France Part 2 Gr. 7-8 |
| SSA1-10 | New Zealand Gr. 4-8 |
| SSN1-51 | Newspapers Gr. 5-8 |
| SSN1-47 | No Word for Goodbye NS Gr. 7-8 |
| SSPC-03 | North American Animals B/W Pictures |
| SSF1-22 | North American Natives Gr. 2-4 |
| SSN1-75 | Novel Ideas Gr. 4-6 |
| SST1-06A | November JK/SK |
| SST1-06B | November Gr. 1 |
| SST1-06C | November Gr. 2-3 |
| SSN1-244 | Number the Stars NS Gr. 4-6 |
| SSY1-03 | Numeration Gr. 1-3 |
| SSPC-14 | Nursery Rhymes B/W Pictures |
| SSN1-12 | Nursery Rhymes Gr. P-1 |
| SSN1-59 | On the Banks of Plum Creek NS 4-6 |
| SSN1-220 | One in Middle Green Kangaroo NS 1-3 |
| SSN1-145 | One to Grow On NS Gr. 4-6 |
| SSB1-27 | Opossums Gr. 3-5 |
| SSJ1-23 | Ottawa Gr. 7-9 |
| SSJ1-39 | Our Canadian Governments Gr. 5-8 |
| SSF1-14 | Our Global Heritage Gr. 4-6 |
| SSH1-12 | Our Neighbourhoods Gr. 4-6 |
| SSB1-72 | Our Trash Gr. 2-3 |
| SSB1-51 | Our Universe Gr. 5-8 |
| SSB1-86 | Outer Space Gr. 1-2 |
| SSA1-18 | Outline Maps of the World Gr. 1-8 |
| SSB1-67 | Owls Gr. 4-6 |
| SSN1-31 | Owls in the Family NS Gr. 4-6 |
| SSL1-02 | Oxbridge Owl & The Library Gr. 4-6 |
| SSB1-71 | Pandas, Polar & Penguins Gr. 4-6 |
| SSN1-52 | Paperbag Princess NS Gr. 1-3 |
| SSR1-11 | Passion of Jesus: A Play Gr. 7-8 |
| SSA1-12 | Passport to Adventure Gr. 4-5 |
| SSR1-06 | Passport to Adventure Gr. 7-8 |
| SSR1-04 | Personal Spelling Dictionary Gr. 2-5 |
| SSPC-29 | Pets B/W Pictures |
| SSE1-03 | Phantom of the Opera Gr. 7-9 |
| SSN1-171 | Phoebe Gilman Author Study Gr. 2-3 |
| SSY1-06 | Phonics Gr. 1-3 |
| SSN1-237 | Pierre Berton Author Study Gr. 7-8 |
| SSN1-179 | Pigman NS Gr. 7-8 |
| SSN1-48 | Pigs in Literature Gr. 2-4 |
| SSN1-99 | Pinballs NS Gr. 4-6 |
| SSN1-60 | Pippi Longstocking NS Gr. 4-6 |
| SSF1-12 | Pirates Gr. 4-6 |
| SSK1-13 | Place Value Gr. 4-6 |
| SSB1-77 | Planets Gr. 3-6 |
| SSR1-74 | Poetry Prompts Gr. 1-3 |
| SSR1-75 | Poetry Prompts Gr. 4-6 |

| Code # | Title and Grade |
|---|---|
| SSB1-66 | Popcorn Fun Gr. 2-3 |
| SSB1-20 | Porcupines Gr. 3-5 |
| SSR1-55 | Practice Manuscript Gr. Pk-2 |
| SSR1-56 | Practice Cursive Gr. 2-4 |
| SSF1-24 | Prehistoric Times Gr. 4-6 |
| SSE1-01 | Primary Music for Fall Gr. 1-3 |
| SSE1-04 | Primary Music for Spring Gr. 1-3 |
| SSE1-07 | Primary Music for Winter Gr. 1-3 |
| SSJ1-47 | Prime Ministers of Canada Gr. 4-8 |
| SSK1-20 | Probability & Inheritance Gr. 7-10 |
| SSN1-49 | Question of Loyalty NS Gr. 7-8 |
| SSN1-26 | Rabbits in Literature Gr. 2-4 |
| SSB1-17 | Raccoons Gr. 3-5 |
| SSN1-207 | Radio Fifth Grade NS Gr. 4-6 |
| SSB1-52 | Rainbow of Colours Gr. 4-6 |
| SSN1-144 | Ramona Quimby Age 8 NS 4-6 |
| SSJ1-09 | Ranching Community Gr. 3-4 |
| SSY1-08 | Reading for Meaning Gr. 1-3 |
| SSN1-165 | Reading Response Forms Gr. 1-3 |
| SSN1-239 | Reading Response Forms Gr. 4-6 |
| SSN1-234 | Reading with Arthur Gr. 1-3 |
| SSN1-249 | Reading with Canadian Authors 1-3 |
| SSN1-200 | Reading with Curious George Gr. 2-4 |
| SSN1-230 | Reading with Eric Carle Gr. 1-3 |
| SSN1-251 | Reading with Kenneth Oppel Gr. 4-6 |
| SSN1-127 | Reading with Mercer Mayer Gr. 1-2 |
| SSN1-07 | Reading with Motley Crew Gr. 2-3 |
| SSN1-142 | Reading with Robert Munsch 1-3 |
| SSN1-06 | Reading with the Super Sleuths 4-6 |
| SSN1-08 | Reading with the Ziggles Gr. 1 |
| SST1-11A | Red Gr. JK/SK |
| SSN1-147 | Refuge NS Gr. 7-8 |
| SSC1-44 | Remembrance Day Gr. 1-3 |
| SSPC-23 | Reptiles B/W Pictures |
| SSB1-42 | Reptiles Gr. 4-6 |
| SSN1-110 | Return of the Indian NS Gr. 4-6 |
| SSN1-225 | River NS Gr. 7-8 |
| SSE1-08 | Robert Schuman, Composer Gr. 6-9 |
| SSN1-83 | Robot Alert NS Gr. 4-6 |
| SSB1-65 | Rocks & Minerals Gr. 4-6 |
| SSN1-149 | Romeo & Juliet NS Gr. 7-8 |
| SSB1-88 | Romping Reindeer Gr. K-3 |
| SSN1-21 | Rumplestiltskin NS Gr. 1-3 |
| SSN1-153 | Runaway Ralph NS Gr. 4-6 |
| SSN1-103 | Sadako & 1000 Paper Cranes NS 4-6 |
| SSD1-04 | Safety Gr. 2-4 |
| SSN1-42 | Sarah Plain & Tall NS Gr. 4-6 |
| SSC1-34 | School in September Gr. 4-6 |
| SSPC-01 | Sea Creatures B/W Pictures |
| SSB1-79 | Sea Creatures Gr. 1-3 |
| SSN1-64 | Secret Garden NS Gr. 4-6 |
| SSB1-90 | Seeds & Weeds Gr. 2-3 |
| SSY1-02 | Sentence Writing Gr. 1-3 |
| SST1-07A | September JK/SK |
| SST1-07B | September Gr. 1 |
| SST1-07C | September Gr. 2-3 |
| SSN1-30 | Serendipity Series Gr. 3-5 |
| SSC1-22 | Shamrocks on Parade Gr. 1 |
| SSC1-24 | Shamrocks, Harps & Shillelaghs 3-4 |
| SSR1-66 | Shakespeare Shorts-Perf Arts Gr. 1-4 |
| SSR1-67 | Shakespeare Shorts-Perf Arts Gr. 4-6 |
| SSR1-68 | Shakespeare Shorts-Lang Arts Gr. 2-4 |
| SSR1-69 | Shakespeare Shorts-Lang Arts Gr. 4-6 |
| SSB1-74 | Sharks Gr. 4-6 |
| SSN1-158 | Shiloh NS Gr. 4-6 |
| SSN1-84 | Sideways Stories Wayside NS 4-6 |
| SSN1-181 | Sight Words Activities Gr. 1 |
| SSB1-99 | Simple Machines Gr. 4-6 |
| SSN1-19 | Sixth Grade Secrets 4-6 |
| SSG1-04 | Skill Building with Slates Gr. K-8 |
| SSN1-118 | Skinny Bones NS Gr. 4-6 |
| SSB1-24 | Skunks Gr. 3-5 |
| SSN1-191 | Sky is Falling NS Gr. 4-6 |
| SSB1-83 | Slugs & Snails Gr. 1-3 |
| SSB1-55 | Snakes Gr. 4-6 |
| SST1-12A | Snow Gr. JK/SK |
| SST1-12B | Snow Gr. 1 |
| SST1-12C | Snow Gr. 2-3 |
| SSB1-76 | Solar System Gr. 4-6 |
| SSPC-44 | South America B/W Pictures |
| SSA1-11 | South America Gr. 4-6 |
| SSB1-05 | Space Gr. 2-3 |
| SSR1-34 | Spelling Blacklines Gr. 1 |
| SSR1-35 | Spelling Blacklines Gr. 2 |
| SSR1-14 | Spelling Gr. 1 |
| SSR1-15 | Spelling Gr. 2 |
| SSR1-16 | Spelling Gr. 3 |
| SSR1-17 | Spelling Gr. 4 |
| SSR1-18 | Spelling Gr. 5 |
| SSR1-19 | Spelling Gr. 6 |
| SSR1-27 | Spelling Worksavers #1 Gr. 3-5 |
| SSM1-02 | Spring Celebration Gr. 2-3 |

| Code # | Title and Grade |
|---|---|
| SST1-01A | Spring Gr. JK/SK |
| SST1-01B | Spring Gr. 1 |
| SST1-01C | Spring Gr. 2-3 |
| SSM1-01 | Spring in the Garden Gr. 1-2 |
| SSB1-26 | Squirrels Gr. 3-5 |
| SSB1-112 | Stable Structures & Mechanisms 3 |
| SSG1-05 | Steps in the Research Process 5-8 |
| SSG1-02 | Stock Market Gr. 7-8 |
| SSN1-139 | Stone Fox NS Gr. 4-6 |
| SSN1-214 | Stone Orchard NS Gr. 7-8 |
| SSN1-01 | Story Book Land of Witches Gr. 2-3 |
| SSR1-64 | Story Starters Gr. 1-3 |
| SSR1-65 | Story Starters Gr. 4-6 |
| SSR1-73 | Story Starters Gr. 1-6 |
| SSY1-09 | Story Writing Gr. 1-3 |
| SSB1-111 | Structures, Mechanisms & Motion 2 |
| SSN1-211 | Stuart Little NS Gr. 4-6 |
| SSK1-29 | Subtraction Drills Gr. 1-3 |
| SSY1-05 | Subtraction Gr. 1-3 |
| SSY1-11 | Successful Language Pract. Gr. 1-3 |
| SSY1-12 | Successful Math Practice Gr. 1-3 |
| SSW1-09 | Summer Learning Gr. K-1 |
| SSW1-10 | Summer Learning Gr. 1-2 |
| SSW1-11 | Summer Learning Gr. 2-3 |
| SSW1-12 | Summer Learning Gr. 3-4 |
| SSW1-13 | Summer Learning Gr. 4-5 |
| SSW1-14 | Summer Learning Gr. 5-6 |
| SSN1-159 | Summer of the Swans NS Gr. 4-6 |
| SSZ1-02 | Summer Olympics Gr. 4-6 |
| SSM1-07 | Super Summer Gr. 1-2 |
| SSN1-18 | Superfudge NS Gr. 4-6 |
| SSA1-08 | Switzerland Gr. 4-6 |
| SSN1-20 | T.V. Kid NS. Gr. 4-6 |
| SSA1-15 | Take a Trip to Australia Gr. 2-3 |
| SSB1-102 | Taking Off With Flight Gr. 1-3 |
| SSN1-259 | Tale of Despereaux Gr. 4-6 |
| SSN1-55 | Tales of the Fourth Grade NS 4-6 |
| SSN1-188 | Taste of Blackberries NS Gr. 4-6 |
| SSK1-07 | Teaching Math Through Sports 6-9 |
| SST1-09A | Thanksgiving JK/SK |
| SST1-09C | Thanksgiving Gr. 2-3 |
| SSN1-77 | There's a Boy in the Girls... NS 4-6 |
| SSN1-143 | This Can't Be Happening NS 4-6 |
| SSN1-05 | Three Billy Goats Gruff NS Gr. 1-3 |
| SSN1-72 | Ticket to Curlew NS Gr. 4-6 |
| SSN1-82 | Timothy of the Cay NS Gr. 7-8 |
| SSF1-32 | Titanic Gr. 4-6 |
| SSN1-222 | To Kill a Mockingbird NS Gr. 7-8 |
| SSN1-195 | Toilet Paper Tigers NS Gr. 4-6 |
| SSJ1-35 | Toronto Gr. 4-8 |
| SSH1-02 | Toy Shelf Gr. P-K |
| SSPC-24 | Toys B/W Pictures |
| SSN1-163 | Traditional Poetry Gr. 7-10 |
| SSH1-13 | Transportation Gr. 4-6 |
| SSW1-01 | Transportation Snip Art |
| SSB1-03 | Trees Gr. 2-3 |
| SSA1-01 | Tropical Rainforest Gr. 4-6 |
| SSN1-56 | Trumpet of the Swan NS Gr. 4-6 |
| SSN1-81 | Tuck Everlasting NS Gr. 4-6 |
| SSN1-126 | Turtles in Literature Gr. 1-3 |
| SSN1-45 | Underground to Canada NS 4-6 |
| SSN1-27 | Unicorns in Literature Gr. 3-5 |
| SSJ1-44 | Upper & Lower Canada Gr. 7-8 |
| SSN1-192 | Using Novels Canadian North Gr. 7-8 |
| SSC1-14 | Valentines Day Gr. 5-8 |
| SSPC-45 | Vegetables B/W Pictures |
| SSY1-01 | Very Hungry Caterpillar NS 30/Pkg 1-3 |
| SSF1-13 | Victorian Era Gr. 7-8 |
| SSC1-35 | Victorian Christmas Gr. 5-8 |
| SSF1-17 | Viking Age Gr. 4-6 |
| SSN1-206 | War with Grandpa SN Gr. 4-6 |
| SSB1-91 | Water Gr. 2-4 |
| SSN1-166 | Watership Down NS Gr. 7-8 |
| SSH1-16 | Ways We Travel Gr. P-K |
| SSN1-101 | Wayside Sch. Little Stranger NS 4-6 |
| SSN1-76 | Wayside Sch. is Falling Down NS 4-6 |
| SSB1-60 | Weather Gr. 4-6 |
| SSN1-17 | Wee Folk in Literature Gr. 3-5 |
| SSPC-08 | Weeds B/W Pictures |
| SSQ1-04 | Welcome Back – Big Book Pkg 1-3 |
| SSB1-73 | Whale Preservation Gr. 5-8 |
| SSH1-08 | What is a Community? Gr. 2-4 |
| SSH1-01 | What is a Family? Gr. 2-3 |
| SSH1-09 | What is a School? Gr. 1-2 |
| SSJ1-32 | What is Canada? Gr. P-K |
| SSN1-79 | What is RAD? Read & Discover 2-4 |
| SSB1-62 | What is the Weather Today? Gr. 2-4 |
| SSN1-194 | What's a Daring Detective NS 4-6 |
| SSH1-10 | What's My Number Gr. P-K |
| SSR1-02 | What's the Scoop on Words Gr. 4-6 |
| SSN1-73 | Where the Red Fern Grows NS 7-8 |
| SSN1-87 | Where the Wild Things Are NS 1-3 |

| Code # | Title and Grade | Code # | Title and Grade | Code # | Title and Grade | Code # | Title and Grade |
|--------|-----------------|--------|-----------------|--------|-----------------|--------|-----------------|
| SSN1-187 | Whipping Boy NS Gr. 4-6 | | | | | | |
| SSN1-226 | Who is Frances Rain? NS Gr. 4-6 | | | | | | |
| SSN1-74 | Who's Got Gertie & How...? NS 4-6 | | | | | | |
| SSN1-131 | Why did the Underwear ... NS 4-6 | | | | | | |
| SSC1-28 | Why Wear a Poppy? Gr. 2-3 | | | | | | |
| SSJ1-11 | Wild Animals of Canada Gr. 2-3 | | | | | | |
| SSPC-07 | Wild Flowers B/W Pictures | | | | | | |
| SSB1-18 | Winter Birds Gr. 2-3 | | | | | | |
| SSZ1-03 | Winter Olympics Gr. 4-6 | | | | | | |
| SSM1-04 | Winter Wonderland Gr. 1 | | | | | | |
| SSC1-01 | Witches Gr. 3-4 | | | | | | |
| SSN1-213 | Wolf Island NS Gr. 1-3 | | | | | | |
| SSE1-09 | Wolfgang Amadeus Mozart 6-9 | | | | | | |
| SSB1-23 | Wolves Gr. 3-5 | | | | | | |
| SSC1-20 | Wonders of Easter Gr. 2 | | | | | | |
| SSB1-35 | World of Horses Gr. 4-6 | | | | | | |
| SSB1-13 | World of Pets Gr. 2-3 | | | | | | |
| SSF1-26 | World War II Gr. 7-8 | | | | | | |
| SSN1-221 | Wrinkle in Time NS Gr. 7-8 | | | | | | |
| SSPC-02 | Zoo Animals B/W Pictures | | | | | | |
| SSB1-08 | Zoo Animals Gr. 1-2 | | | | | | |
| SSB1-09 | Zoo Celebration Gr. 3-4 | | | | | | |